Captain Billy's Whiz Bang

America's Magazine of Wit, Humor and Filosophy

WINTER ANNUAL EDITION

October 1, 1921 Vol. III. No. 26

Published Monthly 13 Issues a Year W. H. Fawcett, Rural Route No. 2 Robbinsdale Minnesota

Entered as second-class matter May 1, 1920, at the postoffice at Robbinsdale, Minnesota, under the Act of March 3, 1879

Price, One Dollar

$3.50 a Year for 13 Issues

"We have room for but one soul loyalty and that is loyalty to the American people.—Theodore Roosevelt.

Facsimile edition
published 2014
About Comics

Edited by a Spanish and World War Veteran and dedicated to the fighting forces of the United States

Table of Contents

In addition to a variety of jokes, stories, jests, jingles and Smokehouse poetry, we offer for your special approval the following:

Table of Contents Continued on Next Page

Table of Contents--Continued

Drippings From the Fawcett

TWO years ago Captain Billy's Whiz Bang exploded pedigreed bunk, junk or whatever you might wish to call it, with the idea in mind that Ye Editor might be able to inject a little more humor into our rural community of Robbinsdale. The printer told us it would be as cheap to print 5,000 magazines as it would to print 100 or so, which was the number we planned to distribute among our friends just returned from service in the army, navy and marine corps.

And so, under the exuberant "exuberation" of "exubrious" raisin juice we generously permitted the printer to turn out 5,000 of our first issue. After giving away a couple of hundred among our friends around Robbinsdale we were puzzled what to do with the remaining 4,800. Mrs. Bill suggested that we send them out around the country rather than build a bonfire, and so I borrowed the Hotel Red Book directory and during leisure hours after milking the cows and salting down the horses, we addressed free copies to a couple hundred hotel news stands around the country. And imagine our joy and manifest surprise when checks began to come back to our rural mail box.

Our receipts the first month were seventy-eight dollars, and thus encouraged, we decided to be "generous" once more. With the November, 1919, issue, we printed 3,500 copies and sold virtually every one of them. A couple months later, through the good offices of the Independent Magazine Distributors' Association and Mr. B. A. McKinnon, of the Pictorial Review, we obtained lists of news dealers throughout the country, and began a small circular campaign from the Whiz Bang farm house.

We were crude, and perhaps because of our unfamiliarity with the magazine distributing business, we attracted the attention of various news dealers around the country. In February of 1920, we received our most pleasant shock —a letter from one "Cohen News Company, 30 Vessey Street, New York," ordering 5,000 copies monthly from us. Up went the circulation to 30,000!

Thus encouraged, we sent out more circular letters to newsdealers, but four months later the "Cohen News Company" disappeared, together with $4,000 worth of magazines. We had to mortgage the old homestead to meet the loss. It was tough pickin's but somehow or other we didn't lose heart and stuck to the game.

In October, 1920, we celebrated our first birthday by calling the October issue our Winter Annual and printing several thousand more books than our usual order. We put in a few such masterpieces as "The Girl in the Blue Velvet Band" and stories from our earlier issues. The result was astonishing. The Annual sold out on the Pacific coast within a few days and within a couple of weeks not a copy could be found at any news stand in the United States.

We celebrated our success in the proper manner in Minneapolis, and over-bubbling with enthusiasm—inspired and otherwise—we called up the printer and told him to run 90,000 copies of the next issue. When we sobered down a few days later, we regretted our hasty judgment, but again we were surprised with a clean sale.

Since then it has been the same story over and over again and now the old Whiz Bang is soaring onward to the million mark monthly.

To the hundreds of thousands of loyal readers we extend a heartfelt thanks and to the thousands of friendly news dealers we only say we wish we could visit each and every one of you on the day the United States goes wet again and with our foot alongside of yours on the brass rail, bend our elbows and say "Here's how!"

For the benefit of the new readers we will repeat our opening explanation for our existence on this mundane sphere, as originally published in our first issue.

Whiz-z Bang!!! We're off and in our trail follows a mighty explosion of pedigreed bull. "Make it Snappy" is our motto. Snap! Pep! Ginger! Even more. The first issue of CAPTAIN BILLY'S WHIZ BANG is off the press and with its advent the editor and contributors hope to have added something really worth while to brighten the atmosphere of human existence. Captain Billy's only

and original WHIZ BANG will explode in every issue. No "duds" allowed in our monthly Literary Indigestion. Today we are the Cherry Sisters of journalism with the fond hopes for "Big Time" sometime.

As the old saying goes, "Laugh and the world laughs with you, near beer and you drink alone." If we dance we must pay the jazz band; no matter what we get we must "put up or shut up." Doctors of Dope and Doctors of Divinity must have the price of our life and love and the undertaker smiles with a self-satisfied grin as our mortal flesh and bones are delivered to the charnel house.

Therefore, the motto of the WHIZ BANG will be: Be happy while you live; live a full life and while you are living, live on the square so you may be able to follow that quaint western philosophy and look every man in the face and tell him to go to Hell.

Please do not get the impression from the title page that the Whiz Bang is to be a military publication only. There will be 100 laughs for the service man and 97¼ laughs for the civilian. We will give the soldier, sailor and marine the benefit of two and three-quarters per cent because we believe he is fairly entitled to it. (Brewers please note.)

THE WHIZ BANG is only in its infancy, so look for the November issue. Then we will burst out and explode into a full-grown bull. We will be fatter, lovelier, snappier and juicier and—oh, girls, we just hate to tell you. Watch for Mr. November and see if we don't make Bill Bryan's Commoner drier than an Algerian caravan in the Sahara desert, twenty miles from the oasic grog shop and the Cliquot Special two weeks overdue. The bull is only half grown and he surely will be some lively animal next month when we sling him over to our readers.

Those of us who have lived through the past five years have the satisfaction of knowing that we have seen the mightiest and most stirring five years in history, and we are watching from day to day the unfolding and ending of the colossal drama. Never has there been such a crashing of empires, such a falling of thrones, such righting of wrongs and deliverance of the oppressed, such vivid demonstration of the wickedness, the folly and the weakness, the nobility, the wisdom and the courage of which human nature is capable.

As a grand finale, an alleviation from the terrific strain, Billy's WHIZ BANG will come as a relieving Balsam—an ointment on the checkered skein of life. Please remember that the oldest truths are the freshest. They are rich with the blood of humanity. As the apple tree in your yard may be a sprout from the apple tree in the Garden of Eden, so the idea that just came to you may be the same that struck King Solomon.. Thoughts are deciduous, as trees, and appear green and fresh to each generation and like desert soil, we are unfurrowed and unfettered.—THE EDITOR.

* * *

(*From an Early Whiz Bang*)

A FEW days ago, for the first time in many moons, I heard sweet strains of "Sweet Adeline" coming in a rich soprano, with bass accompaniment, from a passing automobile on the Whiz Bang farm trail, and it brought me out of my reveries and revived memories of bygone days.

Thoughts of the many times I had heard that song along the trail from town, just after the bars of Robbinsdale and Casey's roadhouse would close, came to me sweetly.

This brand of choral singing has become a lost art under prohibition. "Sweet Adeline" as sung by a troop of celebrators who wouldn't know whether they were standing on their feet or their heads, was very beautiful.

To enjoy it thoroughly, one had to be quite drunk himself. Jack would sing the tenor, Bob the bass and I would join in the chorus, in sentimental strain. It was all very touching. With it, nothing can compare .

In my memories I can still picture Jack's tenor squawking "You're the flower of my heart" and Bob's bass refrain "Sweet Adeline," after which came the grand finale. Ah, those were the happy days.

* * *

WELL, we've still got that automobile seat which the couple left at the Whiz Bang farm several months ago, while they went to town to report the theft of their automobile. So many people seem to have lost seats that we have had dozens of calls for it, but their identification has been imperfect, so we still have the seat.

* * *

Gloomy Reflections

Did you ever stop to think as the hearse rolls by,
That sooner or later both you and I
Will travel along in the selfsame hack,
With never a worry about coming back?

They'll lift you out and they'll lower you down,
The men with their shovels will stand around;
They'll throw in some dirt and they'll throw in some rocks,
And it will fall with a thump on your old pine box.

The worms crawl out and the worms crawl in,
They'll crawl all over your mouth and chin;
They'll call in their friends and their friends' friends, too,
And you'll look like hell when they're through with you.

* * *

A FEW years ago while visiting in Minneapolis I met a philosophical chap by the name of Leo Barrett. Barrett invited me to a nearby club for a "wee bit." Here was his philosophy: "Bill, I feel guilty today. Such a beautiful, sunshiney Sunday afternoon and I had such a 'hangover' this morning that I did not attend church.

"But, on second thought, Bill, I should not feel so bad. Do you know that when I passed the Y. M. C. A. building on Tenth Street this morning, I gazed at the cornerstone and read thereon this inscription: 'Jesus Christ, the cornerstone of this building.' That made me feel remorseful. But I walked a few feet farther to a bicycle rack for the same building and this is what I read: 'Always Keep Your Bicycles Locked.' Then, somehow or other I was glad I didn't go to church. Somebody might have stolen the watch my mother gave me."

Some philosophy, I claim.

* * *

THIS writing finds me closer to church than I have been in many years. Went to an institution, sanitarium, hospital or likker relief cure, or whatever you may want to name it. Kinda wanted to be prepared for a dry New Year, jagtime? I was there just three days when I took the third degree, or lost a calf, or went over the top, or whatever the 'ell they call it in these institutions. During the process I could hear the chanting of that familiar Sunday School song: "Happy Day, Happy Day, When Nursie Took My Calf Away." Oh, it's great, boys.

Soon I'll have the diploma and then the gosh darned cows down on the Robbinsdale farm will "ketch" the dickens. No more will I say: "It has the smell, and kicks like hell, but tastes like rotten glue."

But nevertheless, Old John Barrelhouse Barleycorn will ever have a strong exponent in the skipper. The poor old man is down and out now, apparently, so why kick him. Wait for the day of resurrection, and in the meantime lay off the "junk." Camels are bad enough.

She's a great game, if you don't weaken.

* * *

(*From the Whiz Bang of May, 1921*)

OUT on Rural Route No. 2 we haven't much class, as the saying goes, but we have a lot of fun. We haven't any bright lights, although the folks about the country have bought so liberally of my little bundle of bunk lately that I have been able to put in a small farm lighting plant in the Whiz Bang house, barn and yard.

Not many Minnesota farmers can afford, in these low-wheat-price days, such a luxury as an electric lighting plant, and so the one put in at the Whiz Bang farm created quite an interest.

Gus, our hired man, thought it would be a good idea to have a sort of celebration over the new electric lights. The idea met with instant approval from Mrs. Bill and the kids. The next question was how to celebrate the great event. Gus suggested a "snoose" party, but as not all of my neighbors chew the Copenhagen breakfast food, his suggestion received a cool reception, particularly from Mrs. Bill, who dislikes the habit. It was left to my twelve-year-old daughter to solve the problem, later in the day, when I discovered her in the loft of the old red barn practicing toe dancing. This suggested to my mind a dancing party.

And so we gave the party. I wired the hay loft with electric lights and dumped a pail full of oatmeal on the floor to make it slippery. We picked Gus as the dance master, and here was his predominating action for the evening:

On a balmy night, when the weather's clear,
The boys and girls from far and near;
We'll congregate on the Whiz Bang farm,
To cut some capers in the old red barn.

We have a drum and a jew's harp, too,
Jim Moss plays on the tin bazoo;
And a fiddler over from Sugar Creek—
Pick 'em up Silas and lay 'em down deep.

Oh, we'll dance all night to the latest tune,
The Maiden's Prayer or the old Hip Croon;
We'll walk the dog and ball the jack,
And promenade around the old hay stack.

The horses nicker and the roosters crow,
Balance all and away you go;
Dance that one step nice and clean,
Possum trot and the lima bean.
Now swing around like the old barn door,
If the music stops, then holler "more."
Oh, pinch your gal on her rosy cheek—
Pick 'em up Silas and lay 'em down deep.

Pick 'em up Silas and lay 'em down deep,
Ain't no game of hide and seek,
Pick them knot holes from the floor,
Change your partners, forward four;
Hear the music to your feet,
Pick 'em up Silas and lay 'em down deep.

The only fault we had to find with Gus' musical attainments was that he didn't say anything about the dingbusted lighting plant going on the blink during the dance. Something went wrong and the lights went out, and when we came to again, I was horrified. Mrs. Bill says we can't give any more dances; not if those girls from Sugar Creek are allowed to attend.

* * *

DOC GRAVES, my trained dentist, and myself quite often make an economic tour of investigation on behalf of the price commission division of the Modern Amalgamated and Protective Order of Bohemian Booze Hounds. It is some lodge, and Doc is some gurgler when gurgling, just as he is some tooth extractor when he gets his old stump puller in working condition.

But what I started in to say was that when we had quite thoroughly investigated the fluctuating prices of various brands of "kill-'em-quick," the doctor ventured the assertion that only two things in the world caused insanity. One, he said, was the bum liquor the bootleggers peddle now-a-days, and the other the rotten teeth to which mankind quite often falls heir.

To strengthen his argument, the Doc told a story of a man who became violently insane about a year ago.

"He was so weak in his upper story that he drew an immediate passport to the Anoka bughouse," he said. "The medical authorities of the hospital for the insane found their new patient suffering from focal infection caused from a dozen or two badly decayed molars. The patient was permitted to return to Minneapolis, in the custody of relatives, who delivered him to my office for treatment. I yanked the decayed stumps and the man immediately became mentally normal."

His interesting story appealed to me so strongly that I questioned the good doctor further.

"Say, Doc," sez I, "what's this fellow doing now?"

"Oh, hell!" laughingly spluttered the Doc, "he went insane again when he received my bill."

* * *

"Our Daily Prayer"

Our Father who art in Washington,
Put us wise to the game;
Give us this day our monthly pay,
And forgive of all our fines and stoppages,
And lead us into privations
And deliver us from the loan shark,
And those who want to take away
Our twenty per cent, double time, five cents a mile, etc.,
For thine is the United States, Alaska and Panama,
The Philippines and Hawaii, forever and ever, Amen.

* * *

Oh, Doctor!

The sleeping sickness is bad enough;
The talking sickness worse,
But the drinking sickness sure is tough
On a guy with a slender purse.

* * *

Many a bachelor has made a number of women happy by not marrying them.

Tarnished Goods

Here I stand upon a new threshold
Of life's whirling, restless stream,
Stand at the place where I so often
Hoped for yes, and dreamed
Of the lover, manly, clean and true,
Filled with higher plans of life
Than I ever knew,
And I what am I?
      Tarnished goods.

Sometimes an arm around my waist
Sometimes like tired children rest,
For my heart craved for sympathy
And I laid my head upon a boyish breast;
Little by little I drifted down life's stream,
Little by little I lost the maiden's flush
That puts the sparkle in life's stream,
Till all modesty was lost
And I was,
      Tarnished goods.

For there comes to me a man
Fit in all ways to be a woman's mate,
I beat life's cage with tired wings
And murmur at my fate,
That I must face it all, the deceit,
The false life, and see the pain,
That will bring lines of sorrow
And change of hearts,
This love will never be mine again,
      God pity Tarnished goods.

* * *

A clergyman was dining in a west end restaurant one evening, when a woman wearing a bareback gown entered and took a seat at the next table. The padre could not help overhearing some remarks by the lady about his personal appearance. He took no notice until the waiter offered him some mayonnaise with his salad.

Then he said in his blandest pulpit voice:

"No, thanks; I don't require dressing, but I think the lady at the next table does."

Under Weepin' Willows

EACH spring and summer for the past five years I had visited with them during a two weeks' fishing trip, and they had always been glad to see me.

The little cabin clinging precariously to the rocky shoulder of Little Turkey-Track Mountain was a wonderful spot to me, where I could sit in the dusk and watch the shadows deepen farther up the valley; while down among the willows along the most wonderful trout stream in the world, the fireflies cut sudden glowing figures in the velvet darkness.

She was a shy little bird-like woman with eyes of a beautiful soft brown like a doe in early spring, and there were tiny little love-wrinkles that chased each other about her face when she smiled or spoke, and after the evening meal we would sit on the porch of the little mountain shack and talk.

At least I would do the talking and they would listen and he would point my discourse with a "Hum-m" of interest or a "You don't say" of surprise, his kind old face alight with something besides the mere joy of living and hearing of the big things that were doing in the hustling town far down the valley.

And she would sit beside him and sway

gently back and forth in the old cane-bottom chair and I'd see his gnarled old hand steal softly out and rest lovingly on her withered palm where it lay on the arm of the rocker, and the soft look in her eyes would grow more soft, more luminous, and she'd bring her gaze back from the purple-shadowed valley and her eyes would rest on his and I'd catch a glimpse of that shy, wrinkly, little smile.

This year I made the trip as usual, although the weather was bad, and I glimpsed the little cabin through a cold driving mist at the end of a long wet day, and as I came to the foot of the steep path leading up from the trail, I saw the old man standing in the door shading his eyes with his hand. I waved to him and caught his answering signal before I began the climb.

He came down off the porch to meet me and help with my fishing-gear, and was very near me before I lifted my eyes from the slippery path, but the moment I looked up I knew something was amiss.

"Where's Mother?" I asked.

A queer wounded look came into his eyes as they met mine, but he said nothing, then just shook his head a little and reached to help me with my things.

We piled everything on the porch and I turned to take a look at the valley just then filling up to the brim with purple shadow that deepened to black farther up under the Horn of Camel-back Mountain.

Then he began to talk in a thin haunting

voice, and this is what he told me as the day died and the wind came up to sweep away the last of the mist and the moon crept sadly over Old Baldy:

I guess you wondered why
It is
I don't smile so readily no more
Or if I do
Taint happy and free
But kinda sad and grim like
And full o' things
That never was before
Not filled with sunshine
And gladness like it used to be
You see
We been together a long time
A long time her an' me
An' got used to each other's ways
You know
Happy an' all
Sunshine and rain
We used to say
Twant so bad
We had each other
Her an' me
An' now she's gone
She aint here no more
An' I aint much good
Course there's things got to be done
The chores
Cut the wood an' the like
The habits o' forty year or more
Don't change in a week or a day
Though I do bungle 'em right smart
Cause my mind seems far away
Not just down there in the willers
But out past all the world
With her
Bed-time comes
Like always
But to me it's only night
When th' crickets chirp
Through th' evenin' stillness
An' I'm lonesome
Lonesome for a sight o' her
Sittin' there
In that old cane-bottom rocker
Like she always used to be

Just her
An' me
We used to watch
Th' sunsets her an' me
Just sittin'
Hand in hand
While daylight drooped
From bright red gold
And darkness filled the land
But the darkness didn't hold no terrors
'Cause she was here
You see
Now
There's only me
Somehow
I can't seem to feel just right
Her out there alone
Where th' Weepin'-willers
Cast their purple shadows
Through th' night
Life or death
Don't mean much
I say
When you've lost a pal
A life-time pal
Who knows all
Your mean little ways
'An still loves you
That was her
An' the wind in the willers
Is whisperin'
Kiplin's line
She sleepin' out an' far tonight
But not too far
Maybe
Not too far.

* * *

Johnny Get Your Gun

Magistrate: "What is the charge?"

Policeman: "Intoxicated, your Honor."

Magistrate (to prisoner): "What's your name?"

Prisoner: "Gunn, sir."

Magistrate: "Well, Gunn, I'll discharge you this time, but you mustn't get loaded again."

A Drummer's Prayer

Oh Lord, look with a forgiving eye, we beseech thee, on the buyers who lie to us about the low prices our competitors give them; Lord, soften the hearts of the buyers who as soon as they see a drummer, get as busy as a hen with one chicken and keep us standing around until our feet warp and then buy as much as two dollars and sixty-five cents worth and want that billed out the first of next month. Good Lord, curb our tendency to flirt with the married women; the single ones don't count, and they expect it. Teach us not to complain at the roller towels that the multitude has used before we get there. Lord, give us digestions like alligators, that we may well digest the loin steaks cut from the neck where the yoke worked. Teach us to be thankful for the stump-water served us and called coffee. Toughen our hides, that we may sleep soundly in hotel beds already inhabited. Cause us to look with charitable eye on our competitors, who are a sorry lot anyway. Lord, soften the heart of our employers, that they may render us what little commission is due us in full. Oh Lord, teach our wives patience, so they won't expect our wages until we get them. We beseech thee, Oh Lord, to overlook our absentmindedness when we get away from home and forget about being married, and in conclusion, we beg thee, when we have made our last trip, please don't send us below. We have had our part of that place here on earth. Amen.

What in 'ell Was It?

They stood in the London zoological gardens puzzled before a bird.

"It's a heagle," said one.

"It's not; it's a howl," said the other.

They appealed to a bystander.

"Both wrong," he said. "It's an awk."

* * *

You're a "Used to Was"

"My jolly good fellow," said Health, "now you really
Have lately been drawing on me rather freely,
Who riots with Pleasure by night and by day
Must expect that in time there'll be something to pay.
For the favors you've had, that you may not forget,
Suppose you just give me your note for the debt,
Write as I dictate:
"Twenty years after date,
I promise to pay to my health, sure as fate,
For value received, in sin, folly and pleasure,
These prominent parts of estates I should treasure:
My limbs to be racked with rheumatics and gout;
My teeth to decay till they mostly rot out;
My eyes to grow dim and my hair to grow gray,
While dropsy and asthma take turns day by day;
My nerves and my lungs, too, together give way;
My stomach to fall to dyspepsia a prey;
My taste to forsake me, my voice to grow weak,
While my ears cannot hear, save when conscience shall speak.
Now sign it. When due you need not waste your breath
For extension. Remember, the protest is Death."

* * *

The Kiss

The kiss is a peculiar proposition, no use to one, yet absolute bliss to two; the small boy gets it for nothing, the young man has to steal it, and the old man has to buy it.

It is the baby's right; the lover's privilege; the hypocrite's mask. To a young girl, Faith; to a married woman, Hope, and to an old maid, Charity.

Fable of the Bull

Reprinted from March, 1920, issue

ONCE upon a time there was a Bold Knight, Sir Billy, who loved a Lady Fair, and, like all Knights so Bold, he bethought himself that he would pursue something Elusive; accomplish something to elevate Himself in the Esteem of the Lady Fair.

Now it so happened that there was inscribed upon the Records of the Jockey's Bible an Old Legend of a Great Man whose fame as the Keeper of the Pedigreed Bull had spread far and wide, but that one day his Famous Animal had wandered away, and Behold, for all time since, it had been the Burning Desire of all Knights Bold to find its hiding place. Though many had gone in quest of this Strange Creature, few had returned. Many had thrown this Bull, but few had made it Stick-thrown.

"Verily, I shall capture this Pedigreed Bull," quoth he, "And will throw him in a million pieces throughout the whole Wide World."

"Yea Bo," quoth the Lady Fair, "Do that little thing for me."

And so it came to pass that the Bold Knight set forth. On the seventh-eleventh day he reached Golden Valley, where strange dialects were spoken and odors of Lutefisk reached his Nostrils.

"At last," quoth the Bold Knight, "This is Robbinsdale, Minnesota." And just then a Yokel appeared on the road.

"Me good friend," quoth Sir Billy, "Can you direct me to the Pedigreed Bull?"

"Ay can do dat," quoth the Yokel. "Right over har in de pasture."

And it came to pass that Sir Billy found the Pedigreed Bull and with his trusty WHIZ BANG, threw him to the four corners of the earth—and made him Stick-thrown.

MORAL: If you must throw the Bull, make him Stick.

* * *

Did It Ever Happen to You?

A pretty girl sat in a railroad train,
  As lonesome as she could be;
And she said to herself with a little sigh,
  "If he'd only talk to me."

The young man sat just across the aisle,
  From the girl with the pretty stare,
And he said to himself, "If I sit with her,
  I wonder if she would care?"

And so they rode the whole long day,
  And neither one of them knew
Just what the other was thinking of.
  Did it ever happen to you?

* * *

Regular Jazz Babies

Two young ladies were standing on the sidewalk listening to a minstrel show band playing some jazz. There were two men working in a trench near them, unknown to the ladies. One of the ladies turned to her companion and said, "If they keep up this music I am going to take off my coat and shimmy."

The two men working in the trench overheard her and one of them said, "Boy, if she does I am going to take off my jumper and overalls."

* * *

A Candid Witness

In the examination of an Irish case for assault, counsel on cross-examining one of the witnesses asked him what they had at the first place they stopped at. He answered:

"Four glasses of ale."

"What next?"

"Two glasses of wine."

"What next?"

"One glass of brandy."

"What next?"

"A fight, of course!"

* * *

It Is Not a Custom, I'm Told

Here's a maiden's answer to "Maybe You Do, but I Doubt It."

When you stroll all alone 'neath a clear summer sky,
With a gentleman handsome and bold.
Do you shove him away when he hovers too nigh?
It is not the custom I'm told.

When he holds your hand in his masterful grasp,
Pretending to save it from cold.
Do you tell him to stop with a horrified gasp?
It is not the custom I'm told.

When he presses a passionate kiss on your lips,
Much sweeter than those that are sold.
Do you quit him and let him go off in a "tiff"?
It is not the custom I'm told.

The Whiz Bang Bug Test

Nutty Ned, psychological examiner for Co. P. S. O. L. unit of 250 men, leaned forward majestically, punctuating his remarks with a lurid yellow pencil.

"Now, when I say 'go,' go; and when I say 'stop,' stop."

Prior to his remark, the class of potential imbeciles, who had visions of two golden shave-tail bars, had been cautioned not to cheat, and not to ask the teacher to leave the room.

A tragic silence hung like a shroud over the mess hall. The very atmosphere was charged with deep thought emanating from the puerile and impuerile minds of the wondering "near looies." "Go!" clanged the examiner, and the gallop was on.

Turning the pages right side up they beheld the first question—squares, triangles, rectangles, circles, etc., jumbled together and interlocking like a Chinese puzzle.

The instructions read as follows: Insert the letter 'A' in that part of the square which is in the rectangle but not in the parallelogram, triangle or circle; the letter 'B' in that part of the circle which is in the square and the parallelogram but not in the rectangle or triangle; the letter 'C' in that part of the parallelogram which is in none of the other figures, and the letter 'D' in that part of the circle which is in all the other figures. Finally insert a double XX in any part of any figure which has the same area as a correspondingly dissimilar, but, nevertheless, equal part of any other figure.

"Time allowed for this question, five seconds."

Having triumphantly completed the first question, the class passed on to No. 2, reading as follows:

"If you were bathing in the Y. W. C. A. tank with Annette Kellermann, Lydia Pinkham, Eva Tanguay and Jeannette Rankin, and you saw three men sinking in a tub, and at the same time you were bitten on the leg by a mermaid, would you

1. Present arms?
2. Light a pipe?
3. Kill the mermaid?
4. Get some pink pills for pale people?
5. Telephone your wife?
6. Ask for a newspaper?

And now we have the third question, short but sweet:

"Is Billy Sunday a

1. Grave Digger?
2. Lion Tamer?
3. Bull Slinger?
4. Croquet Player?
5. Disease?
6. Scented Soap?
7. Odor?
8. Hot-house Plant?

Here is the last question. Doughboys, what's your answer?

"If you appeared at retreat without rifle, belt and bayonet ,and the captain chanced to notice your carelessness, would you:

1. Smile sweetly and say: "I'm so sorry, but I forgot the damn piece."

2. Swipe the rifle belonging to the man next in ranks?

3. Tell the captain you'll skin back to the orderly room and get it?

4. Glare haughtily at the captain and say: 'Sir, I gave it to the first sergeant for long arm inspection?' "

As the result of the above examination, 10 men of the unit were found to be insane, 25 were morose, 16 were imbeciles, 2 normal and the balance feeble-minded.

* * *

Clip This Out

I have been bawled out, balled up, held up and held down,
Bulldozed, black-jacked, walked on, cheated, squeezed and mooched,
Stuck for war tax, excess profits tax, state tax, dog tax and syntax,
Liberty Bonds, Baby Bond and the bonds of matrimony,
Red Cross, Green Cross, and the double cross.
Asked to help the society of St. John the Baptist,
G. A. R., Woman's Relief Corps, men's relief, and stomach relief.
I have worked like the devil and have been worked like hell;
Have been drunk; and have gotten others drunk.
Last of all I had to part with my furniture,
And because I won't spend or lend all of the little I earn,
And go beg, borrow or steal,
I have been cussed and discussed, boycotted, talked to and talked about,
Lied to and lied about, held up and hung up,
Robbed and damn near ruined,
And the only reason I am sticking around now,
Is to see what in the Hades is coming next.

Did You Ever?

A furrier was selling a coat to a woman customer. "Yes, Ma'am," said he, "I guarantee this to be genuine skunk fur that will wear for years."

"But suppose I get it wet in the rain?" asked the woman. "What effect will the water have on it? What will happen to it then? Won't it spoil?"

"Madam," answered the furrier, "I have only one answer: Did you ever hear of a skunk carrying an umbrella?"

* * *

Dear Mabel

They met at a dance. He was tall and stalwart, she—oh, so sweet.

They jazzed, they one-hopped, they two-whirled, they—well, they did just what everybody's doin' now.

After the seventh dance with his charmer the young fellow stopped suddenly and glanced suspiciously around.

"It's funny, Mabel," he said. "See that glum looking chap over here. He's been following us about all the time. Who is he and what's he after?"

"Who—that miserable, half-starved fellow in the spotted red tie?" remarked Mabel, casually. "Don't worry about him; he's only the fellow who paid for me to come in."

* * *

The hand that cooks the meal is the hand that rules the world.

Silenced Him

William S. Morris, Jr., was defending one party to an auto collision and was cross-examining a lady witness who was undeniably pretty.

"Have you any idea what caused this accident?" thundered Bill.

"I think so," said the fair witness.

"Then tell the court how it happened," thundered Bill, eager for the facts.

"Must I tell the truth?"

"You have sworn to do so."

"Well, sir, I was standing on the corner, and that gentleman turned to look at something and ran into the other machine."

"Ah," divined the astute William S., "he turned to look at you. That makes you an accessory before the fact, madame."

"I—I think it was the—the accessories he was looking at," murmured the witness.

* * *

Little Miss Muffet
Sat on a tuffet
Drinking a bowl of whey,
A friend put a stick in it,
Making a kick in it.
The end of a perfect day'

* * *

Another Cock-eyed Yarn

She—"George, dear, you have such charming eyes."

He (proudly)—"Oh, is that so?"

She—"Yes, they are always looking at each other."

The Man Hater

I WILL not be weak. I will never fall in love. I will remember that men are without conscience or charity. I will forbid myself the association of men, or the acquaintance of men. I hate men. I hate them.

I hate the way they stare. I hate the thoughts I read in their eyes. There was one on the street car today—a type. I felt as if I were a cat, and my fur bristling at the sight of him. Another spoke to me as I left. I wished then that I were a cat, with claws and teeth. If all the men in the world except my father were driven out and killed that would be better—it would be a happy place. Now, I guess I am a cat.

Is there to be any relief ever? Am I always to be haunted and watched? Who was it wrote about the Alaskan dog being watched greedily and hungrily by team-mates, ready to tear it to pieces when it falls from exhaustion? Are men like that? I believe it. Man is like a blind dog in a meat house.

* * *

First Black Lady—"Dat baby ob yours am de puffec image of his daddy."

Second Black Lady—"He suah am. He am a reg'lar carbon copy."

Nonsense, Larry

The next picture, ladies and gentlemen, is that of the Rocky Mountain goat. You can't get this goat's goat because he leaps from precipice to precipice and back to crag again. And every time he leaps he grunts and every time he grunts he leaps.

—Turn the crank, Larry.

The next picture is that of the laughing hyena which is the species of animal life that made the wild cat wild. The laughing hyena eats only once a week and drinks once a year, so I don't see whyinel he laughs so much.

—Turn the crank, Larry.

* * *

Only Plain Bunk

Now this flower of stockyards fragrance
  Does not bloom alone for men,
Women use it to advantage
  In their business now and then;
If you cop a handsome fairy,
  When the lights are burning bright,
And the horse of dawn is riding
  Down the beaten tracks of night;
And she lisps her baby crooning,
  Tells you you're her darling skunk;
Boys, hike right away to mother,
  For she's handing you plain bunk.

* * *

"Isn't our pitcher grand," exclaimed the enthusiastic young lady at the ball game. "He hits their bats no matter where they hold them."

Hunting the Wily Pole Cat

(As told by a French-Canadian)

I'm hunt de bear, I'm hunt de rat,
Sometimes I'm hunt de cat;
Las week I'm tak ma ax an go
To hunt de skunk pole cat.

Ma fren Bill says hees ver good fur,
Same time good for eat,
So I tell ma wife, "I get fur coat
Same time get some meat."

I walk, one, two, three, four mile,
I feel one awful smell—
I theenk that skunk hees gone and died
And fur coat's gone to hal.

Bime-by I get up ver ver close,
I raise ma ax up high—
Dat gaddum skunk he up and plunk,
Trow something in ma eye.

Sacre, blue; I tink ahm blin—
Gee Cri! Ah cannot see,
Ah run aroun and roun and roun
Till bump in gaddum tree.

Bime-by I drop de ax
An light out for de shack,
I tink about a milyun skunk
Hees climb upon ma back.

Ma wife she meet me at de door,
She sick on me de dog,
She say, "You no sleep here tonight,
Go out and sleep wit hog."

I try to get in hog pen,
Gee Cri, now what you tink,
Dat gaddum hog no stan for dat
On account of awful stink.

So I no hunt de skunk no more
To get hees fur and meat;
For if hees breath he smell so bad,
Gee Cri! what if he speet.

* * *

If a woman is thin, she can fix it some way, but there is no hope for the fat ones.

A Tragedy

An actress died.
Her admirers sighed.
The manager swore and the ladies cried.
Then to an undertaker they did go,
And bought a casket, white as snow.
They next turned their attention to the decorations,
Which the undertaker said, depended entirely on the deceased's relations.
If to the altar she was never led
Deck her in white from foot to head,
But if a married life has been her fate,
Pale heliotrope is the shade in which to decorate.
The ladies paused, then made reply,
"All in pure white, yet let us fondly hope,
That you will place—well—just here and there,
A dash of heliotrope."

* * *

Our Heavenly Wireless

Mike died and went to heaven, while his pal, Pat, joined the Spiritualists and got in communication with his late lamented partner.

"How do you like it up there in heaven?" Pat asked over the spirit wireless.

"Foine," replied Mike. "We have plenty to eat and drink and all of the pennies are worth a million dollars and every minute is a thousand years."

"Mike, lend me a penny, will yez?"

Over the spiritual line came Mike's ghostly reply, "All right, Pat, in a minute."

The Wedding of the Persian Cat

A Persian kitty, perfumed and fair,
Strayed out through the kitchen door for air,
When a Tom cat, lean and lithe and strong,
And dirty and yellow came along.

He sniffed at the perfumed Persian cat,
As he strutted about with much eclat,
And thinking a bit of time to pass,
He whispered: "Kiddo, you sure have class."

"That's fitting and proper," was her reply,
As she arched the whiskers over her eye,
"I'm ribboned, I sleep in a pillow of silk
And daily they bathe me in certified milk."

"Yet we're never contented with what we've got,
"I try to be happy, but happy I'm not,
"And I should be joyful, I should, indeed,
"For I certainly am highly pedigreed."

"Cheer up," said the Tom Cat, with a smile,
"And trust your new found friend a while.
"You need to escape from your back yard fence;
"My dear, all you need is experience."

The morning after the night before
The "Cat Came Back" at the hour of four;
The look in her innocent eyes had went,
But the smile on her face was the smile of content.

And in the after days when children came
To the Persian kitty of pedigreed fame,
They weren't Persian—they were black and tan,
And she told them their pa was a traveling man.

* * *

Sam's Girl

By Charles C. Walts.

Sam's girl is tall and slender;
My girl is fat and low.

Sam's girl wears silks and satins;
My girl wears calico.

Sam's girl is swift and speedy;
My girl, demure and good.

Do you think I'd swap for Sam's girl?
You know darn well I would!

Why Is It?

Why is it the tenderest feet must tread the roughest road?
Why is it the weakest back must carry the heaviest load?
While the feet that are surest and firmest have the smoothest paths to go,
And the back that is straightest and strongest has never a burden to know.

Why is it the brightest eyes are the ones soon dimmed with tears?
Why is it the lightest heart must ache and ache for years?
While the eyes that are hardest and coldest shed never a bitter tear,
And the heart that is meanest and smallest has never an ache to fear.

Why is it those who are saddest have always the gayest laugh?
Why is it those who need not have always the biggest half?
While those who know never a sorrow have seldom a smile to give,
And those who want just a little must strive and struggle to live.

Why is it the sweetest smile has for its sister—a sigh?
Why is it the strongest love is the love we always pass by?
While the smile that is cold and indifferent is the one for which we pray,
And the love we kneel to worship is only common clay.

Why is it the noblest thoughts are the ones that are never expressed?
Why is it the grandest deeds are the ones that are never confessed?
While thoughts that are like all others are the ones we always tell,
And the deeds worth little praise are the ones that are published well.

Why is it the friends we trust are the ones who always betray?
Why is it the lips we wish to kiss are the ones so far away?
While close by our side (if we knew it) is a friend who loyal would be,
And the lips we might have kissed are the lips we never see.

Why is it the things we all can have are the ones we always refuse?
Why is it none of us live the lives (if we could) we'd choose?
While the things we can all have are the ones we always hate,
And life seems never complete no matter how long we wait.

(A Workhouse Prisoner in Washington Times.)

Bargain Day

Two darkies were suing for divorce. It was necessary for the old parson who had married them to testify. He appeared, and this colloquy ensued:

Judge: "Parson, what's your name?"

Parson: "William Lewis, C. W. B. M., youh honah."

Judge: "Do you know this couple?"

Parson: "Yas, suh."

Judge: "Did you marry them?"

Parson: "No, suh!"

Judge: "Didn't marry 'em? Why, they have proof you did."

Parson: "Mebbe, so, boss, but yo' see it was lak dis: Dat yaller Moses come to me an' said he'd gib me two dollars to marry him. I sez, 'All right,' and he went and got that ole woman and brung her to de church. Just efo' de ceremony he 'low as how he ain't got but six bits to gib me. Boss, I couldn't puhfohm no reg'lar ceremony like dat for a measly six bits, so I just read de Christian Endeavor pledge ober dem and turned un loose."

* * *

"Pooh, pooh, my dear man! That is nothing!" he cried. "You should see my place with all the latest improvements. Why, my patients nearly always ask me to send a message to fetch a photographer so they can be photographed with the expression of gladness which my patent dental treatment alone can give them."

A Sad Battle

I witnessed two soda jerkers in a little boxing match recently.

They were both good "mixers." It was just a one round affair. The fight by rounds:

Round 1—Soda Squirt No. 1 gave No. 2 a "pop" in the eye. The latter retaliated with a "peachy punch" to the "coke." The crowd gave No. 1 the "raspberry" as he phizzed out for the count. His seconds threw in a couple of straws trying to make it a "draw." But he was dinged up so bad that today he is near bier.

* * *

Pat's Quick Mind

Pat and Mike were working on a new building. Pat was laying bricks and Mike was carrying the hod. Mike had just come up to the fourth floor when the dinner whistle blew.

"I hate to walk down," he said.

"Take hold of this rope," said Pat, "and I'll let you down." Pat let him down half way and then let go of the rope. Mike landed in a mortar bed, not much hurt but terribly angry.

"And why did ye let go of the rope?" he demanded.

"I thought it was going to break," said Pat, "and I had presence of mind enough to let it go."

* * *

The mother of the expert accountant gazed fondly at her son.

"And to think that I have nursed an adder at my breast," she murmured.

Movie Dog Days

BY RICHMOND

THESE are sort of dog days in movieland. Some of the studios are closed, others mostly shut down and a general reduction of forces everywhere. Many a shiny big car, not paid for, has gone back to whence it came, namely, the agent.

The dour ides of the grasshopper days are here. Those who soaked not away when the soaking was good are trying to soak everything in sight, right now. The nightly revelries at Sunset Inn, The Green Mill, The Midnight Frolics and the Cinderella roof go on, but there is not the lavish expenditures of two years ago.

Men who were pulling down a thousand a week, more or less, are walking the streets of Hollywood, wondering how long it's going to last. Things are down to brass tacks right now. The situation is not unexpected. There was over-production of pictures and so much money tied up in unused film that the money bags closed up for the time being.

Without giving Los Angeles any particular credit it may be truthfully said that there is no city in the country which presents such a daily spectacle of feminine pulchitudininity. That's some word, isn't it? May be bad grammar at that. But you get the meaning.

From every city in the country, perhaps the globe, have come thousands of young women with ravishing eyes and wondrous forms. Just where they all get by in the eating line passeth understanding because there is very, very little work for extras today as compared with a year or so ago. Few of these young beauties possess brains enough to be anything but an extra.

It is not so easy to get a job on mere looks. In the upper reaches of filmdom, stern business men are demanding results and less flirtation. The larger studios are less and less permitting Bacchanalian activities such as used frequently to be in order. A higher grade of director is coming into vogue, especially as a result of the tightening up. Those who are retained in pictures today are pretty much needed and have an eye to business.

We are not stating that picturedom has reached a state of chemical purity. Nay, nay, Paula, but men and women both are becoming wiser to the fact that the old game must be played not so strongly if played at all, and with more finesse.

In other words, the picture people are poorer today than they used to be, but they are longer on experience. Also many of them are burned out in more ways than one. When the game gets going again the entire business will be on a stronger and cleaner basis.

* * *

When the stove pipe fell, the soot followed suit.

"Life's a Funny Proposition"

Many requests from Whiz Bang readers for the publication of "Life's a Funny Proposition After All," the famous recitation by George M. Cohan, are answered herein. The Whiz Bang has obtained the original recitation and permission to publish it from the author.

Did you ever sit and ponder
Sit and wonder
Sit and think
Why we're here and what this life is all about?
It's a problem that has driven many brainy men to drink,
It's the weirdest thing they've tried to figure out,
About a thousand theories all the scientists can show
But never yet have proved a reason why
With all we've thought and all we're taught
Why, all we seem to know is we're born
And live a little while
And then we die.
Life's a very funny proposition after all.
Three meals a day
A whole lot to say,
When you haven't got the coin
You're always in the way.
Everybody's fighting as we wend our way along,
Every fellow claims the other fellow's in the wrong.
Hurried and worried until we're buried
And there's no curtain call,
Life's a funny proposition, after all.
When all things are coming easy and when luck is with a man,
Why, then life to him is sunshine everywhere;
Then the Fates blow rather breezy and they quite upset a plan,
Then he'll cry that life's a burden hard to bear.
Though today may be a day of smiles,
Tomorrow's still in doubt
And what brings me joy may bring you care and woe.
We're born to die.
But we don't know why
Or what it's all about,
And the more we try to learn the less we know
And no one's ever solved the problem properly as yet.
Young for a day, then old and gray,
Like the rose that buds and blooms
And fades—and falls away.
Losing health to gain our wealth
As through this dream we tour,
Everything's a guess and nothing's absolutely sure.
Battles exciting and fates we're fighting
Until the curtains fall,
Life's a funny proposition, after all.

Doubts Dispelled

"What's happened to Blondie all of a sudden?" asked Claudine of the rapid-fire restaurant. "She's been in the indigo for days, but now she's as chirky as a medder lark."

"She's satisfied about Spike," replied Heloise of the same establishment. "She asked him on the street last night if he really and truly loved her, and he slapped her jaw right in front of a picture show for having any doubt of it."

* * *

Sunday Church a la Blue Law

The announcement on the bulletin board.

The pained expressions.

The awakening by the church wardens.

The arrival in the church patrols.

The dry lunch.

The drier lecture on "Sabbath"—that day of peace."

The hours of monotony.

The announcement of adjournment by the wardens.

The herding of the thoughtless souls who strayed.

The ride back.

The arrival at home.

The sigh of thankfulness.

The lights put out at 9:00.

The happy dreams of yester-year.

* * *

He: "What do you think of the Ouija board?"

She: "I never stayed at that hotel."

Dream On, Oh Cavalier

What could be more beautiful? Those gentle curves will always be embedded in my memory with such distinctiveness that even Time cannot erase.

Did ever one see such a neck? With its delicate mold it seems almost transparent. Surely the gods must have had no small part in the construction of this beautiful form. Its perfect beauty arouses the poetic instinct within me and as I gaze enrapt my very soul pours out its adoration.

And as the lines slope gently downward and then outward I gaze with expectancy. Farther and farther they form a perfect curve and then —abruptly the lines on both sides turn and the form is perfectly flat on the bottom. In seeking true art one can even find beauty in a champagne bottle.

* * *

Omar Up to Date

Since the eves gone by we spent so gay,
Some long for the booze that was taken away;
But for me I'll be content with just one—
A Whiz Bang and a piece of lawn;
Then I'll build a monument not so high
Which no one shall see but a passerby.

* * *

Gob Lingo

A sea-going gob passed the following remark in a restaurant:

"Gimme a slice of hookum cow, and pass 'em through the galley fast—I like 'em rare."

Fooling Friend Wife

One of San Francisco's high army officers felt he couldn't let a holiday get by without mourning at the bier of alcohol. So into his civies he jumped and stepped out, taking his eighteen-year-old daughter for a companion.

At one of the well known beach resorts the officer ran across a brother navy officer, likewise attired.

"Why, hello, John," cried the second, "you stepping out, too?"

"Oh, yes, got to celebrate, you know."

"Say you ought to see the young chicken I got with me," confided the second as he nudged a little closer." Some pip, I'll say, 'n the wife's away, too. But, say, who's that little infant you're steppin' around with? I'd like to meet her myself."

"Oh, that—that's my daughter," exclaimed the first, nervously and a trifle embarrassed.

"Your daughter! Say, that's a good one. I'm going to tell that myself next time. It's got the cousin stall beat a mile."

* * *

Goosey, Goosey Gander

The Smiths heard Liza Gander, their maid, in the bathroom laughing and giggling for nearly an hour.

"What's so funny, Liza?" asked Mrs. Smith, knocking on the bathroom door.

"Lawsa me," replied Liza between giggles. "Ize so nervous, ah caint dry mesself."

The Girl With the Blue Velvet Band

In that city of wealth, beauty and fashion;
Dear old Frisco, where I first saw the light,
And the many frolics that I had there
Are still fresh in my memory tonight.

One evening while out for a ramble;
Here or there without thought or design,
I chanced on a young girl, tall and slender,
At the corner of Kearney and Pine.

On her face was the first flush of nature,
And bright eyes seemed to expand;
While her hair fell in rich, brilliant masses,
Was entwined in a Blue Velvet Band.

To a house of gentle ruination,
She invited me with a sweet smile;
She seemed so refined, gay and charming
That I thought I would tarry awhile.

She then shared with me a collection
Of wines of an excellent brand,
And conversed in politest language;
This girl with the Blue Velvet Band.

After lunch, to a well-kept apartment,
We repaired to the third floor above;
And I thought myself truly in Heaven,
Where reigneth the Goddess of Love.

Her lady's taste was resplendent,
From the graceful arrangement of things;
From the pictures that stood on the bureau,
To a little bronze Cupid with wings.

But what struck me the most was an object
Designed by an artistic hand;
'Twas the costly "lay-out" of a hop-fiend,
And that fiend was my Blue Velvet Band.

On a pile of soft robes and pillows;
She reclined, I declare, on the floor,
Then we both hit the pipe and I slumbered,
I ponder it over and o'er.

'Tis months since the craven arm grasped me,
And in bliss did my life glide away;
From opium to "dipping" and thieving,
She artfully led day by day.

One evening, coming home wet and dreary,
With the swag from a jewelry store;
I heard the soft voice of my loved one,
As I gently opened the door.

"If you'll give me a clue to convict him,"
Said a stranger, in tones soft and bland,
"You'll then prove to me that you love me."
"It's a go," said my Blue Velvet Band.

Ah! How my heart filled with anger,
At woman, so fair, false and vile,
And to think that I once true adored her;
Brought to my lips a contemptible smile.

All ill-gotten gains we had squandered,
And my life was hers to command;
Betrayed and deserted for another—
Could this be my Blue Velvet Band?

Just a few moments before I was hunted
By the cops, who wounded me. too
And my temper was none the sweetest,
As I swung myself into their view.

And the copper, not liking the glitter
Of the "44" Colt in my hand;
Hurriedly left through the window,
Leaving me with my Blue Velvet Band.

What happened to me I will tell you;
I was "ditched" for a desperate crime;
There was hell in a bank about midnight,
And my pal was shot down in his prime.

As a convict of hard reputation,
Ten years of hard grind I did land,
And I often thought of the pleasures
I had with my Blue Velvet Band.

One night as bed time was ringing,
I was standing close to the bars,
I fancied I heard a girl singing,
Far out in the ocean of stars.

Her voice had the same touch of sadness
I knew that but one could command,
It had the same thrill of gladness
As that of my Blue Velvet Band.

Many months have passed since this happened,
And the story belongs to the past;
I forgave her, but just retribution
Claimed this fair but false one at last.

She slowly sank lower and lower,
Down through life's shifting sands,
'Till finally she died in a hop joint,
This girl with the Blue Velvet Band.

If she had been true when I met her ,
A bright future for us was in store,
For I was an able mechanic,
And honest and square to the core.

But as sages of old have contended,
What's decreed us mortals must stand;
So a grave in the potter's field ended
My romance with the Blue Velvet Band.

Now, when I get out I will hasten
Back to my home town again,
Where my chances are good for some dollars,
All the way from a thousand to ten.

And if I'm in luck I'll endeavor
To live honest in some other land,
And bid farewell to dear old Frisco,
And the grave of my Blue Velvet Band.

* * *

Vy Not?

The Irish lad and Yiddish boy were engaged in verbal combat. First one would insist that his father or mother were better than the other's. Then it was their pet bulldogs and their teachers. Finally the subject came down to respective churches.

"I guess I know that Father Harriety knows more than your Rabbi," the little Irish boy insisted.

"Shure, he does; vy not?" replied the Jew boy. "You tell him everything."

Shakespeare Preferred

"Do you care for Browning?" asked the poetical man with the long hair of the conspicuously dressed newly rich lady at his right.

"Not so loud, please," whispered the woman. "My husband has an awful jealous disposition."

—John Bull Junior.

* * *

Martin (affectionately)—"Mary, dear, I've had something hesitating on my lips for some time and now—"

Mary (interrupting)—"Oh, Martin, how I do hate those little mustaches."

* * *

Sucker to Hawkeye

Here's to the American eagle;
That noble bird of prey;
Who eats his meals in Illinois
And flies to Ioway.

Hawkeye to Sucker

Here's to the state of Ioway,
With virgin soil so tried;
We don't need the word,
Of the American bird,
So tie your bull outside.

* * *

"Come, come," said Tom's father, "At your time of life
There are excuses no longer for playing the rake.
It is time you were thinking of taking a wife."
"Why, so it is, Father; whose wife shall I take?"

The Shooting of Dan McGrew

By Robert W. Service.

From The Spell of the Yukon—By permission of the publishers of Service's works, Barse & Hopkins, 21-39 Division street, Newark, N. J.

A bunch of the boys were whooping it up in the Malemuke saloon,
The Kid that tickled the music-box, was playing a jag-time tune;
Back of the bar in a solo game, sat Dangerous Dan McGrew,
While watching his luck was the light of his love,
The Lady—that was known as Lou.

When out of the night which was fifty below
And into the din and the glare
There stumbled a miner, fresh from the creeks,
Dog-dirty, and loaded for bear.

He looked like a man with one foot in the grave
And scarcely the strength of a louse,
As he tilted a poke of dust on the bar
And called for the drinks for the house.

There was none could place the stranger's face,
Though we searched ourselves for a clew;
But we drank to his health, and the last to drink
Was Dangerous Dan McGrew.

There are men that somehow just grip your eyes
And hold them hard like a spell,
And such was he for he looked to me
Like a man who had lived in hell.

With a face most hair, and a glassy stare
Like a dog whose day is done,
As he watered the green stuff in his glass
And the drops fell one by one.

Then I got to figuring who he was
And wondering what he'd do,
When I turned, and there stood watching him
Was the Lady, who was known as Lou.

The stranger's eyes wandered round the room
And seemed in a kind of a daze,
Till at last that old piano fell
In the way of his wondering gaze.

The Rag-time Kid was having a drink,
There was no one else on the stool,
And the stranger stumbled across the room
And flopped down there like a fool.

In a buck-skin shirt that was glazed with dirt
He sat and I seen him sway,
With a talon hand he clutched the keys;
God, but that man could play.

Were you ever out in the great alone,
When the night was awful clear
And the icy mountains held you in
With a silence that you most could hear?

With only the howl of a timber wolf,
As you camped out there in the cold,
A half-dead thing in a stark dead world
Clean mad, for the muck, called gold.

While high overhead green, yellow, and red,
The Northern lights swept in bars:
Then you have a hunch what the music meant
Hunger night, and the stars.

Hunger, not of the belly kind
That's banished with bacon and beans,
But the gnawing hunger of a lonely man
For a home, and all that it means.

For a fireside far, from the cares that are—
Four walls and a roof above,
But oh, so cram full of cozy joy
And crowned with a woman's love.

A woman dearer than all the world
And true as heaven is true;
God, how ghastly she looks through her rouge
The Lady, who was known as Lou.

The music almost died away, so soft
That you scarce could hear,
And you felt that your life had been looted
Of all that it once held dear.

That someone had stolen the woman you loved
And her love was a devil's lie,
And your guts were gone and the best for you
Was to crawl away and die.

'Twas the crowning glory of a heart's dispair
And it thrilled you through and through.
I guess I'll make it a spread Misere,
Said Dangerous Dan McGrew.

The music almost died away,
Then oft burst like a pent-up flood,
And it seemed to say, repay, repay,
And your eyes went blind with blood.

And the thought came back like an ancient wrong,
And it stung like a frozen lash,
And the lust awoke, to kill, to kill,
And the music stopped with a flash.

The stranger turned and his eyes they burned
In a most peculiar way;
In a buckskin shirt that was glazed with dirt
He sat and I seen him sway.

Then his lips went in a kind of grin
And he spoke, and his voice was strong
And, boys, said he, you don't know me
And none of you care a Damn.

But I want to state, and my words are straight
And I'll bet my poke they're true,
That one of you is a "Hound of Hell"
And that one is Dan McGrew.

Then I ducked my head and the lights went out
And two guns blazed in the dark;
Then the lights went up and a woman screamed,
And two men lay stiff and stark.

Pitched on his head and pumped full of lead
Lay Dangerous Dan McGrew,
While the man from the creeks, lay crushed on the breast
Of the Lady that was known as Lou.

These are the simple facts of the case,
And I guess I ought to know,
They said the stranger was crazed with hooch
And I'm not denying it's so.

I'm not so wise as their lawyer guys,
But strictly between us two,
The woman that kissed him and pinched his poke
Was the Lady, that was known as Lou.

* * *

Speaking of pugilists, Kid McCoy's eighth wife is seeking a divorce. This recalls a once popular saying, 'I love my wife, but oh, you kid!"

Modern Philosophy

We are indebted to a friend for the following clipping which expresses the terms in which a modern advertising concern directs attention to the benefits of its system of advertising and which is worth reading:

"Did it ever occur to you that man's life is full of crosses and temptations? He comes into the world without his consent; goes out against his will, and the trip is exceedingly rocky.

The rule of the contraries is one of the features of this trip. When he is little, the big girls kiss him. When he is big, the little girls kiss him.

If he is poor, he is a bad manager. If he is rich, he is dishonest. If he needs credit, he can't get it. If he is prosperous, everybody wants to do him a favor.

If he is in politics, it is for graft. If he is out of politics, he is no good to the country. If he does not give to charity, he is a stingy cuss; if he does, it is for show.

If he is actively religious, he is a hypocrite. If he takes no interest in religion, he is a hardened sinner.

If he gives affection, he is a soft specimen. If he cares for no one, he is cold blooded. If he dies young, there was a great future before him. If he lives to an old age, he missed his calling.

If you save your money, you're a grouch;
If you spend it, you're a loafer;

If you get it, you're a grafter;
If you don't get it, you're a bum—
So what the hell's the use?
Life is just one thing after another.

Don't marry anything in the world but your wife, and if she is not satisfactory, advertise."

* * *

Our Winter Yarn

A negro from Mississippi was discharged from the army in the north during the winter time and finally wound up in Duluth, Minnesota. With the weather 50 degrees below zero and no work, in his wandering around the streets, he became frozen, and was found by two coppers and taken to the crematory as his last resting place. After placing him in the furnace and awaiting for his carcass to burn up, they prepared to remove his ashes. Upon opening the door, they found him sitting up, cross legged, and with a smile over his face, "Boss, shet that door, da is a heluva draft comin' in."

* * *

Where Is Yours?

A colored parson was reading the Ten Commandments to his congregation, and when he came to the one that is broken more than any other—the one that leads to Reno, a sporty brother in the congregation snapped his fingers and registered an air of satisfaction, then whispered to his neighbor: "Now Ah done know where Ah left mah umbrellah."

Verily, Dat's De Text

There was once a very good negro preacher who had the very bad habit of stealing chickens. One night he was caught leaving a deacon's hen roost with a big fat hen under his arm. The next day he was dismissed from the fold and told to leave the city. He drifted to a distant settlement and once more established himself in a church of his belief.

All went well for a time, nothing being heard from his old church. He was beginning to think that he would never be recognized as the hen roost preacher of former days. But, alas, fate was against him.

The following Sunday he arose to deliver his sermon. As he did so, he adjusted his eyeglasses and surveyed the congregation. As he scanned the row of brothers, who should he spy but Sam Brown from the old church. He knew he had to talk and talk fast. He began his sermon thus:

"Brothers and sisters, I'll not take fo my tex dis morning' what I sed las' Sunday I wus gonna take. Stid o' dat my tex is gwine to be, 'Brother, if'n yo knows me, kepe yo mouf shet, fo verily I will see yo' later.'"

* * *

Her Reference

Lady (to applicant for position of lady's maid): "And have you any references?"

The Applicant: "Non, Madam, but ze husband of ze lady where I worked gave me zis so beautiful wristlet watch."

Evolution

By Langdon Smith.

When you were a tadpole and I was a fish;
In the Paleozoic time;
And side by side, on the ebbing tide,
We crawled through the ooze and the slime
Or skittered with many a caudal flip
Through the depths of the Cambrian fen;
My heart was rife with the joys of life,
For I loved you even then.

Mindless we lived and mindless we loved
And mindless at last we died,
And deep in the rifts of the Carados drifts
We slumbered side by side;
The aeons came and the aeons fled
And the hot-lands heaved amain,
Till we caught our breath from the womb of death
And crept into life again.

We were amphibians, scaled and tailed,
And drab as a dead man's hand;
We coiled at ease, 'neath the dripping trees,
Or crawled through the mud and the sand;
Croaking and blind with our three-clawed feet,
Writing a language dumb,
With never a spark in the empty dark
To hint at a life to come.

Then light and swift through the jungle trees
We flung our airy flights,
Or breathed in the balm of the smouldering palm
In the hush of the moonlit nights.
And Oh, what wonderful years were these,
When our hearts clung each to each,
And the shadows broke, and our souls awoke
In the first faint dawn of speech.

Thus life by life, and love by love,
We passed through the cycles strange,
And breath by breath, and death by death,
We followed the change on change,
Till there came a time in the law of life,
When over the nursing sod,
The shadows broke, and our souls awoke
In a vague, dim dream of God.

I was thewed like an Auroch bull,
And tusked like the great cave bear;
While you, my sweet, from head to feet,

Was gowned in your glorious hair;
Deep in the gloom of a fireless cave,
While the night hung o'er the plain,
And the moon hung red o'er the river bed,
We munched the bones of the slain.

I flaked a flint to a cutting edge,
And shaped it with brutish craft;
I broke a shank from the woodland dank,
And fitted it head and haft;
Then I hid me close to the reedy tarn,
Where the mammoth came to drink;
Through brawn and bone, I drove that stone,
And slew him upon the brink.

Loud I howled through the moonlit wastes,
Loud answered our kith and kin;
From west and east to the crimson feast,
The clans came trooping in;
Through joint and gristle and padded hoof,
We fought and clawed and tore
And cheek by jowl, with many a howl,
We talked the marvel o'er.

I carved that fight on a reindeer bone,
With a rude and hairy hand;
I pictured his fall on the cavern wall,
That men might understand;
For we lived by blood and the might of right,
Ere human laws were drawn,
And the age of sin did not begin
Till our brutal tusks were gone.

And that was a million years ago,
In a time which no man knows;
Yet here tonight, in the mellow light,
We sit at Delmonico's:
Your eyes are as deep as the Devon springs;
Your hair is as dark as jet;
Your time is new, your lives are few;
Your soul untried and yet——

Our trail lies on the Kimmeridge clay,
And the scarp of the Purbec flags;
We have left our bones on the Bagshort stones,
And in the heart of the Coraling crags;
Our love is cold, our lives are old,
And death shall come again;
Shall it come today, what man shall say
That we shall not live again?

God wrought our souls from the Tremadoc beds,
And furnished us wings to fly;
He sowed our spawn in the world's dim dawn,
And I know that we shall not die;
Though cities have grown above the graves,
Where the crook-boned men made war,
And the oxwain creaks o'er the buried caves
Where the mummied mammoths are.

So as we linger at luncheon here,
O'er many a dainty dish,
Let us drink anew to the time when you
Were a tadpole and I was a fish.

* * *

Clearing Up the Difficulty

"Now, my lad," said the police officer, who was investigating the case of a missing check in an office, "I believe you are here first every morning."

"Yes, sir."

"And who is here next—Mr. A. or Mr. B.?"

"Sometimes one, sometimes the other."

"Well, on what days would Mr. A. be likely to get here first?"

"I can't quite say, sir. At first he was always last, but later he began to be earlier, till at last he was first, though before he had always been behind. He was soon late again, though lately he came a bit sooner. Just now he is as much behind as before, but I expect he will come early sooner or later."

"Oh, quite so," said the officer, "that's all I wanted to know."

* * *

The average man spends too much time making money and too little time enjoying it.

By Way of Diversion

Dear Heart, when in your eyes I look to see the lovelight ling'ring there, no artist in the land could paint a picture e'en one-half so fair. I seem to peep into your heart and see my image; round my neck I feel your arms and then, my dear—and then you ask me for a check. Dear heart, when on my brow I feel your hand in gentle, smooth caress, my soul is thrilled in ecstasy; I know not worry or distress. I'm sure that all the world is mine. I dream I wear a kingly crown. 'Tis heavenly and then, my dear—and then you ask me for a gown.

* * *

Creed of the Modern Maiden

(1) To refuse to accept the attention of a man who will not spend a lot of money on me, and to waste no time on those who do not.

(2) To accept everything and give nothing in return.

(3) To be engaged to three men at the same time, on the principle that I can get more from a syndicate than an individual.

(4) To have all men telephone before they call so as to prevent jealousy and to give each the impression that he is "The Only One."

(5) To lose all interest the minute I find a man is in love with me.

(6) To like the army doctor, as he is chased by a lot of married women, as he takes me out to dinners and dances and gives me free medical attendance, though he is eccentric and indifferent.

(7) To show my legs to my knees; to wear my waists cut glaringly low; to smoke cigarettes and drink whiskey, as one knows that this appeals to the animal instincts in men and is the psychology of the demimonde.

(8) To play the "kid part" and thus create the impression that I am in the early twenties when in reality I am nearly forty.

(9) To excite sympathy by my ill health and work my affected accent overtime.

(10) And last, but not least: To hate the man who calls my bluff and wants to marry me.

Toledo Slim

We were seated in a pool room on a cold December day,
Telling jokes and funny stories just to pass the time away;
When the door was softly opened and a form walked slowly in;
All the boys soon stopped their kidding when they saw Toledo Slim.
But a different man was he and they hardly knew the guy;
He no longer wore the glad rags he had worn in days gone by.
He took a look around him as he crept into the place,
And we saw a look of hunger on his dirty, grimy face.
"Hello, Slim, old pal!" said Bosten Red; "you're looking on the pork;
Why, you used to be the swellest guy of any in New York.
Come, tell us, Slim, what happened that you are on the bum?"
The crowd then gathered 'round him and the story Slim begun.

'Tis true I'm on the bum, boys; I'm on the hog for fair.
But in the past I led them all, my roll was always there.
I never turned an old pal down, I spent my money free,
And all the sports along the line were glad to stick with me.
I was an all 'round hustler, I trimmed the birdies right,
I never shied at any game when greenbacks were in sight.
But one sad night I met my fate; I fell like many more,
That's how I'm on the bum, boys, played out and feeling sore;
It happened just five years ago, if I remember right,
I trimmed a sucker for a roll and felt most out of sight.

I took a stroll along the line; "set up" for all the boys,
And just to pass the time away I dropped in Kid McCoy's.
And while I sat there drinking, getting on a mighty stew,
A dead swell dame came in the place and sat beside me, too.
I asked her if she'd have a drink, she sweetly said she would,
And as I gazed into her eyes, I thought I understood.
Perhaps you'll think me fickle, pals, but it isn't any dream;
For when it comes to peachy looks that "Tommy" was the queen.

We "chewed the rag" for quite a while, I "shot the con" for fair,
(And when it comes to spreading salve, you may gamble I was there.)
I told her I would place her in a finely furnished flat,
And when the joint closed up that night I had my girlie pat.
Next day we saw the parson and paid a month's rent down
And then she went a hustling for work around the town.
She'd get up in the morning, go out and get the grub;
While I lay in my downy bed so humble and so snug.
But if the day proved gloomy, then in the house we'd stop.
She'd gather 'round the lay-out while I cooked the fragrant hop.
When winter drew around at last and things were going fine,
We had the swellest flat of any couple on the line.

One night I had a job to do, the richest home in town;
I got my tools and started out with my pal, Jackie Brown.
We never thought we'd get a blow, the thing looked like a pipe,
With all the folks a-sleeping and not a soul in sight.
We put the goods into a sheet and started down the block,
And just as luck would have it we bumped into a cop.
We dropped the swag quick as a flash and started on the run,
With the copper close behind us, a-shooting off his gun.
But we were fleet as greyhounds and were halfway down the street,
When a bullet hit me in the leg and I knew that I was beat.
The copper stopped to handcuff me while Jackie got away,
And I never saw his face again for many and many a day.

Well, boys, I know you'll guess the rest; they made short work of me;
They sent me up the river to do my little "V."
But still I did not worry; I thought my girl would stick
And keep the flat a-going while I did my little trick;
I never thought she'd turn me down in 40,000 years,
But when I think of what came off it almost brings the tears.

At last the long years passed away and one bright summer day,
I started back to old New York so happy and so gay.
But when I reached my little flat I found my girl had flown—
She had run away with Jackie and left me all alone.
It was then I took to boozing and went from bad to worse;
I tried to drown my sorrow and forget the bitter curse,
But my memory of that pretty face was always on my mind,
So I searched the city over, but no trace of her could find.
I roamed the streets at leisure seeking vainly for my prey,
Looking for the man that ruined me and stole my girl away.

I swore that I'd have his life for the trick that he had done,
So I searched the country everywhere, knowing well my time would come.
One day I met a wise guy who knew my pal full well,
He said he was in 'Frisco and living mighty swell.
The girl had died in Denver of consumption, so he said,
Where my former pal had left her to starve from want of bread.
It happened at a time, boys, when I didn't have a cent;
So I beat my way to Frisco with my mind on vengence bent.

One foggy day on Market Street I met him sure as fate;
He tried to get the drop on me, but was a moment late.
I sent a bullet crashing into the traitor's brain,
And then I made my getaway and "glommed" an eastbound train.
That's all there is to tell, boys; I'm like the rest of bums.
I've lost all my ambition and don't care what becomes—
And as he finished talking, from his hip he drew a gun,
In a moment came a sharp report—his grafting days were done.

Our Pedigreed Drama

By W. Worth Bailey II

BUT, Gerald Dear—" Gilda gasped tremulously, as she vainly struggled to release herself from his grasp.

"Now, now. That's all right. Don't worry, no one will ever know."

"But what if any one should come now? Whatever could we do? What could we say?"

"No one will come, dearest. How could any one know that I am here. I am sure no one saw me come in. Come now, be a good, brave little girl."

"Oh, Gerald, please don't kiss me again. You must go, before any one comes," Gilda implored as Gerald gently, but insistently made her sit down on the lounge again. "Please, oh please, dearest, don't—" she gasped as he kissed her passionately.

Then with that she relaxed and lay in his arms, which sinuously twined around the delicate curves of her body. They were still in silent, esoteric adoration while the door of the room opened softly. Suddenly they were rudely aroused from their adoratic embraces by the loud slamming of a door.

"So!—So this is what you are up to while

I am away," a rude voice demanded dramatically.

Gilda turned, gasped, grew pallid and sighed, "My God, my husband."

With that she fainted conveniently in Gerald's arms, who meanwhile was vainly looking for some opening for a hurried exit, and the same time desperately thinking for some valid excuse for his being in that compromising position. He laid Gilda on the lounge and hurriedly made for the door, saying, "I-I'll get her some w-water---"

"Oh, no, you don't," thundered the enraged husband in a stage voice. "None of your sly fox tricks young fellow. I'll have your life's blood for this."

The critic wrote a single word on his cuff, yawned disgustedly at the same old line of melo-drama, turned and left the theatre.

That week the washwoman wondered what on earth the word "Rotten" could mean scrawled on one of the cuffs.

* * *

Winter Sports

Wrestling with the furnace.
Fishing coals out of the sieve.
Camping around the radiator.
Hunting steamer rugs.
Diving between the sheets.
Flying to the bathroom.
Forking farm fertilizer.

The Ace In the Hole

By Al Wilson.

Now you'll meet a lot of guys
Who think they're mighty wise
All because they know a thing or two;
You'll find them every day
Strolling up and down Broadway,
Telling of the wonders they can do;
There's common and there's booters,
There's cardsharps and crapshooters;
They congregate around the Metropole,
They wear flashy ties and collars,
But where'd they get their dollars
If they'd lose that good ace down in the hole?

(Now all join in the chorus)

Some of them write to their old folks for coin;
That is their ace in the hole,
While others skip bells on the old tenderloin;
That is their ace in the hole.
They'll tell you of trips they are going to make
To Italy or the North Pole,
But their names will be mud,
Like a chump playing stud,
If they lose that old ace in the hole.

Now the more you stroll around
In this good old New York town.
You'll find that what I'm telling you is true;
They'll greet you with a smile,
But you'll know all the while,
They're only trying to slip it onto you;
To you they will be telling
Of lemons they are selling,
And money they have spent in buying clothes;
But you know that they are lying,
Its the ace that does the buying,
That clothes them from their heads down to their toes.

* * *

Sunday School Teacher—"We should never do in private what we would not do in public."

Bad Boy—"How about taking a bath?"

* * *

If a teamster would say all the mean things a woman can think of, you'd hear some high-class "cussing."

Mark Twain On Prohibition

Mark Twain says: "I am a friend of prohibition and temperance, and I want it to succeed, but I don't think prohibition is practical. The Germans, you see, prevent it. Look at them. They have just invented a way of making brandy out of sawdust. Now, what chance will prohibition have when a man can take a rip saw and go out and get drunk with a fence rail? What is the good of prohibition if a man is able to make brandy mashes out of the shingles of his roof, or if he can get delirium tremens by drinking the legs off his kitchen table?"

* * *

The Grocer's Love

The grocer loved a charming girl,
As lovely as the day;
He wondered if she'd marry him,
And said "Let SOAP she may."

And straightway to her house he went,
Her lovely face to see,
Exclaiming, "Ah, I know full well
That CHEESE the girl for me."

The girl was very kind and said
That she was very glad
To see him there, and then remarked
What a bad COFFEE had.

And they got most intimate,
And she let him kiss her brow;
But when he spoke of marriage, said,
"O, do not TEAS me now."

* * *

He—You were no spring chicken when I married you.

She—No, I was a little goose.

Golightly Highballs

In the following, Rev. "Golightly" Morrill sums up his impressions of various cities and countries in which his travels have taken him during the past quarter century. The Minneapolis fire-eating preacher has been writing for the Whiz Bang almost since it started as a wee soldier's publication two years ago, and this article consists of excerpts from early issues. Rev. Morrill belongs to the new school of preachers—if you smoke, drink, chew, inhale snoose or flirt with the girlies, he deplores it, but believes in the old adage, "Let your conscience be your guide," and he will tell you that "If you can't be good at least be careful." You will get a hot, tropical "kick" from the "Golightly Highballs."

BY REV. "GOLIGHTLY" MORRILL

Pastor People's Church; Minneapolis, Minn.

Mexico

L. A. in Latin America stands for "licentious animals." In Vera Cruz the principal male pastime is to talk about girls and not of God. From 4:00 P. M. to 2:00 A. M. men sit in the plaza portales drinking, smoking and talking about the women who pass by. The leading subject of "town talk" is girls, the one they went to the movie with last, the other one the night before, and the one they hope to get tonight.

The people make themselves a sewer for immoral filth, court the devil Lust that eats and burns up their blood; are spendthrifts of body and soul; waste their inheritance to purchase dirty, loathed diseases; pawn their bodies to a dry-rot evil; make themselves patients for Lust's rendezvous, a hospital, where their bill of fare is pills, not beef, and the doctor's bill is longer than the moral law they have violated. What I have written here about Vera Cruz morals applies to the rest of Mexico where conditions are the same or worse.

Honolulu

THE Hawaiians are out and out in their dancing. They do not gloss it over, and they wear no hypocritical fig leaves. They do not throw masks or mantles over their viciousness, under the guise of religious charity balls and philanthropic society parties. The hula is a hip dance, but the Hawaiians are not "hip"—ocritical in doing it. The dance is not sad or hippish but one of joy.

I have seen many dances—the Apache in Paris, du centre in Cairo, the can-can in Buenos Aires, and with money here in Honolulu one can arrange with a chauffeur or at a hula house to see a hula combining all these vile and violent exhibitions. It is a composite of the composite of all dirty dances, most delightfully depraved, innocent of decency and shame, the dancers being quite careless about the exposure of their legs, arms and charms. What captivating indelicacy, so disturbing to the lookeron. But this is not the native hula. There is sufficient of the sun and volcano without it. The whites have taken away the native naivete and added their own nastiness. As a physiological study the dance is informing. In antiquity these antics were a religious service, combining poetry, pantomime and passion. The old edition of the heathen hula dance has been expurgated, but Christian foot-notes suggest more.

Havana

HAVANA is a fool's paradise—a lunatic limbo for people with loud clothes, lots of money, loose morals and light heads. It is the place where bad folks go to have a good time. The more disreputable a city is, the more popular it is to high society.

I have visited Havana many times and found the H in its name stood for Hell, not Heaven. On a recent sojourn I asked a traveling companion what the state of religion was and if Havana's morals were improved. "Oh, yes, there has been a great reformation." He had scarcely made this gratifying statement when a young man came up to me and showed some vile postcards and postals which he offered for sale. This did not happen in a side street at night, but in Central Park at noon.

Havana has reformed! The city has no "segregation," but you may walk for miles along streets to the waterfront and find every other house with a seductive senorita at the door or window with extended hand or winsome voice urging you in broken Spanish or English to forsake the counsel of your mother's Bible. Regular saloons and concert halls had scores of the women of the town at the tables sitting with motley men, while glasses clinked and phonographs scratched their screechy music.

Poor pleasure-seekers, whose law is fashion and folly their pursuit! Bubbles on the wave of pleasure, a tracery on the sand which Time's tide will soon erase. Every year the siren voice of Havana calls, "Come in your private yacht on the Gulf Stream of gold; come with full purse and empty head and heart; come, you 'best' society, that you may be seen at your worst; come, all ye who would desert the temple of your mind and soul for this Circe's palace of fleshly pleasures!"

Central America

HAMLET found something "rotten in the state of Denmark," but it was sweet compared with what I discovered in Central America—the land of eruption and corruption, of dirt, disease, destitution, darkness, dilapidation, despots, delay, debt, deviltry and degeneracy, where a conservative estimate makes 90 per cent of the women immoral, 95 per cent of the men thieves, and 100 per cent of the population liars.

Panama

PANAMA is famous for its canal, the wedlock of the oceans, but the city Panama is infamous, knows little of the family word "wedlock" and its red light "Cocoa Light" would make the fabled Daphne Grove wither up with envy. From the first to the fifteenth of each month the United States soldiers receive their pay and spend a large amount of it here in wine, women and song. In this pandemonium of profligacy, one may see, at any hour of the day or night, a brave soldier boy, intoxicated with love or liquor, sitting in a doorway with a half-dressed, bare-legged girl in his lap.

Martinique

MARTINIQUE is the Circe of the Caribbean and many are the boat crews turned into pigs like the sailors of Ulysses. Here pleasure is a riot, idleness a duty and depravity an accomplishment. Fort de France, the capital, loves to dance in private and public. The "Casino" is the largest hall and is open three days a week, Saturday, Sunday and Monday.

The dance gyrations were grotesque and gym-"nasty"-cal. It would make a Bassarid of Bayadere blush. Between dances they tanked up on Thyonian juice, believing with Tibullus: "Let wine celebrate the day; it is no shame to be tipsy on a holiday and to reel and stagger" The place was suffocating—two hundred jammed in a small hall. As they perspired they became glued together in a sort of African cancan. The furnace-like heat and the degeneracy of their actions created an atmosphere of the Infero.

They squeezed and squirmed, writhed and wriggled—no grace, just disgrace. Most of the girls were masked and clad in nighties. One man wore a union suit, only this and nothing more—

Then they started from their places,
Moved with violence, changed in hue,
Caught each other with wild grimaces,
Half invisible to the view,
Wheeling with precipitate paces
To the melody, till they flew,
Hair and eyes and limbs and faces,
Twisted hard in fierce embraces,
Like to Furies, like to Graces.

South Sea Islands

THE Fijian lover, instead of carving the name of his lady-love on the trees, tattoes his name on her hips and arms. In Samoa the natives are not so immoral as unmoral. They keep "open house" literally without window or door, and figuratively, for you are welcome any hour of the day or night. They are most hospitable, and one of their forms of delightful entertainment to the white man is to invite him into their house to spend the night, during which time one of the elder dames rubs his feet, massages his back, sings to him, fans him, or does anything else she thinks necessary for his comfort. The sleeping room illustrates the Moose motto, "One for all and all for one," for boys and girls, men and women, lie down side by side and go to sleep or wake up whenever they want to.

At Apia, Samoa, one night the women pulled off a dance—and most of their clothes—displaying their agility and some other things. They wore a wreath of flowers on their heads and a kind of grass skirt that stopped short of the knee and opened at the side to show the tattoo marks on the hip. The girls' legs, arms, breasts and stomachs were bare and glistening with cocoanut oil. There were shell-beads around their necks and beads of perspiration on their bodies. All that the male dancers had on was a bath towel around their waists. They sat, swayed and swung in their Siva-Siva dance; moved heads, hands and arms to right and left; jumped up with grunts, chants and clapping hands, went through a wild gymnastic performance that represented working, fighting, rowing, courting and loving.

East India

WHEN I stepped into the bath at Durbar, I was "horrified" to find a beautiful Mohammedan maiden standing there before me with nothing on plus a bracelet. In agitation I rang. The master came, and I told him I did not want that woman there with the bath. He seemed surprised, because she was part of it, shrugged his shoulders, ordered her out, and beckoned to two stalwart natives. They seized me, threw me down on the marble, put a wooden pillow under my head, and then splashed, massaged, pounded, twisted and kneaded me, worked my arms like a windmill, rolled me like a log, used me as a punching bag, went through a whole course of gymnasium exercises on me, then grinned and said, "Not finished." I felt I was, when back came the "sweet sixteen" smiling like Spring, and with less covering than September Morn. I sprang up, but she grabbed a towel and basin and laid me low, then soused me and began to put on the finishing touches. In broken English she tried to tell me all her physical, mental and moral charms, which I admitted because she was a woman, but I knew her Koran didn't square with my Old Testament, so thanking her, I fled, like Joseph from Potiphar's wife, to my room, where my guide "Kim" came to the rescue, helped me to dress and rushed me to the train or I might have been there yet.

I entered the Cow Temple, stable of sitting and standing bulls. The bull is a beatified beast. Priests pet him, the godly natives garland his horns and kiss his tail, virgin votaries bathe their hands, beautify their faces and plaster their hair at the live bull's shrine.

South America

AH, THAT last night at Rio de Janeiro. A long walk brought us to a kind of Leceister Square of many theatres. Believing they were all equally good or bad, we entered one and saw and heard a Portuguese comic opera. It was comical to see some of the red light scenes we had just escaped, enacted on the stage. Again we went out of the light into the night, passing through narrow streets of dives brighter and blacker than any we had yet seen. This was the busiest place in Rio. Although it was midnight, an unending stream of humanity poured up and down the walks, the patroling police charging the crowds time and again.

Paris

WOMEN rule. Cherubim of hell, they sit around in scanty costumes that show what they are supposed to hide, and eat and drink, talk and look and leer with a flushed and overwrought animation of mind and body. De Musset's confession is ours, and first astonishment gives way to horror and pity. The masked ball is but the scum of libertinism; the feast is ennui trying to live; the palace of sin is filled with yawning mouths, fixed eyes and hooked hands.

Venezuela

LA GUAYRA senoritas, like the scenery, are wild, beautiful and romantic, though there are many wizened witches, rheumatic, mustachioed and flea-bitten, who make one seasick on land. The local enchantresses give the stranger a good (bad) time—as well as an assortment of souvenirs. These moral lepers are much more dangerous than the physical ones in the big asylum in the outskirts. Gay girls throw kisses to the tenderfoot as he walks the streets—a most sanitary and microbeless pastime.

Here I entered a girls' school where the young misses were learning much and not missing anything, for as a practical object-lesson in physiology a naked little boy had strolled in from the street and was roaming about the room. Some of the citizens are quite devout and show their gratitude to God for his numerous blessings. I passed a saloon bearing the inscription, "Gracios a Dios" (Thanks to God). Thus do the simple-minded people obey the Scriptural command, "In everything give thanks."

At the Hotel Los Banos, Puerto Cabello, one goes in swimming au natural. Many modest maidens are only clad in a blush, making a tableau vivant. Verily, as the guide-book saieth, "The natural beauties of the place are charming."

* * *

When a Feller Needs a Friend

"You ought to have seen Mr. Marshall when he called upon Dolly the other night," remarked Johnny to his sister's young man, who was taking tea with the family. "I tell you he looked fine a-sitting there alongside of her, with his arm—"

"Johnny," gasped his sister, her face the color of a boiled lobster.

"Well, so he did,' 'persisted Johnny. "He had his arm—"

"John," screamed his mother frantically.

"Why," whined the boy, "I was—"

"John," said his father sternly, "leave the room."

And Johnny left, crying as he went: "I was only going to say that he had his army clothes on."

* * *

"What animal makes the nearest approach to man?" asked the teacher.

"The cootie," replied the red-headed boy.

The Ladies—and the Men

Kipling's famous poem and a woman's reply.

THE LADIES.

By Rudyard Kipling.

I've picked up my fun where I've found it,
    I've ranged and I've roamed in my time,
I've had my choice of sweethearts
    And four of them were prime;
One was a half-caste widow,
And one was a woman from Prome,
And one was the wife of a Jamais-de-near,
    And one was a girl from home.

Now, I ain't so much with the ladies,
    But taking them all the way long,
You never can tell till you've tried them
    And then you are like to go wrong.
There are times when I thought that I might have,
    There are times when I knew that I might—
But the more you learn from the yellow and brown
    Will help you a heap with the white.

I was a young one at Oogli,
    Shy as a girl to begin,
But Aggie de Castra she made me,
    And Aggie was clever as sin.
Older than me, but my first one,
    More like a mother she were,
But she taught me the way to promotion and pay,
    And I learned about women from her.

Then I was sent out to Burma,
    Acting in charge of Bazaar;
I got me a tiny lithe heathen,
    From buying supplies off her pa;
Funny and yellow and faithful,
    A doll in a tea cup she were;
We lived on the square like a true married pair,
    And I learned about women from her.

And then I was transferred to Neemah,
    Or I might have been keeping her now;
I got me a shiney she-devil,
    The wife of a nigger at Mow.
She taught me the Gypsy folks' boolee,
    A kind of volcano she were;
She knifed me one night when I wished she were white,
    And I learned about women from her.

And then came home on a steamer,
Along with a kid of sixteen—
A girl from a convent in Murat,
The straightest I ever had seen.
Love at first sight was her trouble,
She didn't know what it were;
I could not do such, for I loved her too much,
So I learned about women from her.

Now, I've picked up my fun where I've found it,
And now I must pay for my fun,
The more you know about the others,
The less you'll settle to one.
And the end of it's sitting and thinking,
And dreaming of hell fire to see,
So be warned of my lot—as I know you will not—
And learn about women from me.

* * *

MEN—A-LA KIPLING.

By Grace Moody.

I've taken my beaux as I've met them;
The tightwads along with the rest,
The smart set's the place you will get them,
All varied, the worst to the best.
I've had them with hair and without it,
I've had them thin, fat, short and tall,
And I'll state now while I am about it,
That I've learned about men from them all.

I went with a stout thirty-sixer,
Who drove his own automobile,
A prince as an exclusive mixer,
A frost on the marrying deal.
He used to beau 'round all the women,
'Til a shoot up one day
Gave the whole thing away,
And I learned about fellows from him.

Then I met a young chap from the Maple Leaf Land,
With a sad and mysterious past;
And we "loved with a love that was more than a love"
But it wasn't a love that would last.
He left me a heart that was broken,
And memories that time can ne'er dim,
He was only a boy and I a new toy,
But I learned about fellows from him.

Then I met one who looked truly sorrowed
With eyes of that heavenly blue;
No money except what he borrowed,

And he never had heard the word true.
He met a grass widow and left me,
For I then seemed prudish and prim,
He went to the bad, spending more than he had,
And I learned about fellows from him.

Next came a youngster, mere baby,
With his amateur heart all athirst;
He's somewhere and thankin, me maybe,
For turnin' him down at the first.
Now he worshipped the ground I was treading,
(I was nearing the thirty year rim)
But he surely was wild,
Called me "baby" and "child,"
And I learned about fellows from him.

I've known all the men in the smart set,
I've been in love often and deep;
And I'm really not ready to part yet
With the knowledge I've managed to reap.
Let others all bow to soft music
And give vow on the altar grim,
I had one who'd flirt,
At the sight of a skirt,
And I learned about husbands from him.

* * *

Dan Cupid

By Walter Wellman.

Dan Cupid is a funny guy, and he makes lots of blunders. Still young folks say they like his way; that he's performing wonders. I've watched the many tricks he's played; I've seen the cunning traps he's laid; I've seen the errors he has made when he goes out and plunders. When father was a little lad, Dan wasn't so sagacious. He wasn't wise to tricks and lies; his manner was more gracious. He didn't teach the girls to vamp, or on a fellow's trail to camp or cast a sly and wicked lamp, or make the girls flirtatious. But Cupid was a younger guy when daddy went a-sporting. Conditions then more favored men; 'twas cheaper going courting. Girls didn't have to advertise or use silk hose to hypnotize; they didn't have to wink their eyes, or go around cavorting.

But things have changed since father's day, and Cupid's in a pickle, and girls demure, without some lure, are scarcely worth a nickel. So Dannie teaches them to flirt; to wear a thin transparent skirt that makes the Johnnies' eyes revert, although he knows they're fickle. It's lucky things are coming down (I now refer to prices) or you would see what styles would be when things have reached a crisis. Why, even now, statistics show Dan often hits a girl too low. But if she's vain, he's made her so. He's taught her all her vices.

* * *

Life's Philosophy

Buy, and the gang will answer,
Sponge, and they stand and sneer,
The revelers' bound to joyous sound,
And shunt for refusing beer.

Be rich and the world will seek you,
Poor, and they turn and go,
You're a mighty good fellow, when you are mellow,
And you're pockets are lined with dough.

Be flush and you're friends are many,
Be broke and you lose them all,
You're a dandy old sport, at twenty a quart,
But not if you chance to fall.

Give praise and the cheers are many,
Squawk, and the boys go by,
Be smooth and slick and the gang will stick
As close as the hungry fly.

There is always a crowd to help you,
A copious draught to drain,
But when the gang goes home, you must bear alone
The harrowing stroke of pain.

One's Company

The mistress beamed patronizingly on the maidservant.

"I'm going to get you another chair for the kitchen, Norah," she said.

"Sure, I don't need it, ma'am," replied the maid of all work.

"But you have only one," the mistress persisted.

"One's enough, ma'am," responded Norah.

"But you have company some evenings, don't you, Norah?" the mistress queried in surprise.

"Only gentlemen, ma'am," Norah replied, dropping her eyes.

* * *

Good Night

You sing a little song or two,
You have a little chat,
You make a little candy fudge
And then you take your hat.

You hold her hand and say "good night,"
As sweetly as you can—
Ain't that a heluva an evening
For a great big healthy man?

* * *

The Well-Behaved Guest

Because her little boy cried at table when he failed to find before him the food he liked, the hostess said, in admonishment, indicating the boy sitting opposite, who was the guest at supper, "See how Claude behaves at table; he doesn't cry and make such a fuss over what's in his plate, do you, Claude?"

"No, ma'am," answered Claude; "my mamma told me to take what I get and say nothing."

The Hooch Cure Blues

BY M. V. SUMNER

Bring me a dry Martini, waiter, and chase it with something that's wet.
I went to a pink tea yesterday and I haven't got over it yet.
I heard they've discovered the North Pole, waiter, Gee, I wish I had it here now,
They couldn't come any too cold for me to put on my aching brow.

'Twas a stormy night at sea, waiter, and the waves ran mountains high,
Personally, I was souzed to the gills and today I am awfully dry.
Yes, 'twas a frightful night on the sea, and many are missing, I think,
But as near as I can remember, I never missed a drink.

The one in blue got my spark, waiter, her side pal got my clock,
Oh, I don't want to know the time, waiter, just lead me down to the dock,
Yes, lead me down to the dock, waiter, for a watery grave I pine,
The place for a man that's pickled is over his head in the brine.

Just tell them I am at the "Murray" cure, waiter, that I died as a hero should;
Up to my neck in the cold old suds, guaranteed drawn from the wood.
Say, after I've sank in the deep, waiter, you'll do me one favor, I hope,
Tell 'em if I blow up bubbles that 'twasn't from eating soap.

* * *

For Bible Students Only

It was distinctly promised us, in the first chapter of Genesis, that man was to have dominion over every creeping thing; but we have never yet seen the human being who could get the better of an athletic and mature cockroach.

And the Garden of Eden attitude toward prohibition may be deduced from the name given to the first of all rivers. If you don't believe us, turn to Genesis 11 and see what they called the stream Adam had to drink from. "The name of the first is Pison."

Diary of a Divorcee

Tuesday Morning—How splendid it is to be free again. I feel just as I did the day I was twenty, and knew that in future I could do as I pleased, without caring what anybody said. How foolish a girl is to ever get married. I wonder if I shall ever care for a man again?

Wednesday—I think I shall go away for a few months to let people forget. The men stare at me so impudently. Still, it may be that I merely imagine it. They always have had a habit of turning to look at me. I wonder if I really am very pretty, or if, like every woman, I merely think I am? I am to have my cheque once a month. Just think! Two hundred dollars every four weeks to use as I please. That's twice as much as my allowance was when we were married. What a ripping time I shall have.

Thursday—I met Billy Harding yesterday afternoon. How handsome he looked. I think he turned rather red when we passed each other. It was a shame the way I treated poor Bill when—and then how shall I write of him. He is not my husband now, and so I can't call him Herbert any more, and it seems so foolish to say Mr. Follington. Well, anyway, I wonder how I could ever have imagined him handsomer than Bill? No wonder he was jealous.

I wonder—yes, Bill must care for me still. At least he has had plenty of chances to marry other girls if he wanted to. Oh! dear!

Saturday evening—This has been a dreadful day; I have never been so lonely in my life. The paper says he is going to the Rockies to shoot bears and things. I don't believe he is sorry a bit. What hard-hearted wretches men are! I shall never marry again. Their love lasts only as long as it is a novelty. But a woman never gets over it, no matter what may happen. I wonder if other people ever talk about Bill and me? Oh, if I only had a mother to go to! I can't write any more; the tears insist on coming.

Monday—How splendid the world seems today. I took a walk in the park this morning. Met Bill. We were quite friendly and shook hands. After all, why shouldn't we? He says he walks every morning to keep fit. I think I shall try it. I feel the need of exercise, and I must keep well—now.

Tuesday afternoon—Met Bill again this morning. I asked him to call. I wonder if I ought to have done so—so soon? Will he come? He said he would. But there is the "decree absolute" to be got through. How splendidly the weather has turned out. I have such a strange feeling today. I can't describe it. How glad I am to be free again. I can hardly realize that I'm a girl once more. I wish it were tomorrow morning.

Wednesday—It's cloudy and dismal. I wish I were dead. Met Mrs. Uppingham this morning. She hardly bowed to me. How I should hate myself if I were as fat as she, and had such a "before taking" face. I do believe she shaves. I wonder if Bill went some other way this morning on purpose to avoid meeting me? Oh, well, what do I care? I've told him often enough that he never could be any more than a friend to me now. I hope he remembers it. Still, now that I'm free, it would be rather nice —but, there, I can't write any more now.

Thursday—Met Bill this morning. I'm so glad that Bertie Follington and I parted when we did. Living on together would have meant misery for both of us. Bill was unexpectedly called out of town on Tuesday. He's coming this evening. How strange it all seems, and how the time drags. Dear me, I must change my blouse. This one soils so easily, and I can't afford to have finger marks on it—unless I know they are to be worth while.

Friday—Bill was here last night. He came in after dinner, but I can't think of sitting down and scribbling. I wonder if it is wicked of me to feel so happy today. What a strange feeling comes over me whenever I think of something that may happen, only he seemed to be afraid that I might have witnesses hiding behind the furniture. But he'll get over that, after he has come two or three times.

Monday—Poor old book. I haven't written in you for nearly three months. Herbert returned yesterday. He telegraphed, asking if he may come back to me. Says it was all his fault, and he's sorry. Says we must be married again at once. That's just like him, dear, generous fellow. Most men wouldn't acknowledge they were wrong, as, of course, he was—at least, perhaps—I don't know! I'm sorry for Poor Bill. Have just written to him breaking off our engagement. Hope dear old Herbert will never hear about it. There's the bell!

* * *

Ode to the Girl

Little girl, you are so small,
Don't you wear no clothes at all?
Don't you wear no shimmy shirt?
Don't you wear no petty skirt?

Just your corset and your hose,
Are those all your underclothes?
Little girl, you look so slight,
When I see you in the light.

With your skirts cut rather high,
Won't you catch a cold and die?
Aren't you 'fraid to show your calf?
It must make the fellows laugh.

Little girl, what is the cause?
Why your clothes are made of gauze?
Don't you wear no undervest
When you go out fully dressed?

Do you want to catch the eye
Of each fellow passing by?
Little girl, where is the charm
In your long uncovered arm?

Little girl, your mystery,
Loving charms and modesty,
Are what make us fellows keen
To possess a little queen.

And the "V" behind your neck
Is it for the birds to peck?
Little girl, I tell you those
Are not as nice as underclothes.

Little girl, now listen here:
You would be just twice as dear
If you would cover up your charms—
Neck, back, legs and both your arms.

After the Raid

A raid on the National Dutch Room cabaret in Minneapolis recently, in which two hundred fur-clad women and velvet-pocketed escorts were piled into patrol wagons amid a crashing of hip-pocket glassware, inspired Mr. McKillips to write this poetic story.

By Budd L. McKillips

Listen, dearie, stop your cryin'
'Cause they've locked you in a cell;
Don't make noises like you're dyin';
Oh, I know it's simply hell.

Cryin' dear, won't move the jailer,
Won't make him unlock the door;
Use some rouge, you're lookin' paler;
I've been in these raids before.

Dozen times, I guess, they nailed me
When they used to have a line;
Ward boss always came and bailed me—
Sometimes even paid my fine.

Never mind that "Press" sob-sister,
Dry your eyes and play the game—
Ain't no story—beat it, Mister;
Good Lord, dear, don't give your name.

Don't tell him a damn thing, honey;
Hush now, dear, I know your tale;
Just like me you needed money
And stepped out to grab the kale.

Lost your job, maybe slack season;
Didn't have the price to eat—
Maybe not, but that's the reason
Most girls start to hit the street.

Homeless, hungry, maybe freezin',
Soon you found the business paid,
And there wasn't no slack season
Or no lay-offs in our trade.

Conscience hurt when long-faced preachers
Said as how you'd go to hell?
Dear, the sons of those same teachers
Came to buy the thing you sell.

Just forget those sal'ried prayers
When they tell you all those things,
Tell them that the low-wage payers
Don't help grow no angel wings.

Hush, now, dearie, come on, stop 'er,
Cut the weeps and be a sport,
Fix your hair, here comes a copper
For to take us into court.

See the judge, bet he's been stayin'
Out all night—he's got the jerks;
We're up now—what's that he's sayin'?
Holy Gee, we got the works!

* * *

All She Wanted to Hear

A young lady tripped blithely into the local postoffice.

"I want to know," she demanded with a telltale blush as she handed the postmaster a pink communication addressed to her lover, "how long it will be before I get an answer to this letter."

"That depends," he answered; "if he's in jail they will let him write once a month only; if he's dead broke he'll have to wait till he can earn the price of a stamp, and I have no data on which to base an opinion of his earning capacities. If he's ill in bed he may not care to dictate to a disinterested third party, and if it's smallpox they won't let him write at all; ditto, if he's dead. Then, again, if he's got a new girl—"

At which moment he realized that the young lady had flown.

* * *

Clothes are going up again. They used to make the man, but now they break him.

Mistakes

When the plumber makes a mistake he charges twice for it.

When a lawyer makes a mistake it is just what he wanted, because he has a chance to try the case all over again.

When a carpenter makes a mistake it's just what he expected.

When a doctor makes a mistake he buries it.

When a judge makes a mistake it becomes the law of the land.

When a preacher makes a mistake nobody knows the difference.

But when an editor makes a mistake—Good night!

* * *

The other Sunday evening the minister of a local church was holding forth eloquently, in no wise discouraged by the fact that a prominent city druggist was sound asleep in the front row. The subject for the evening was "Faith," and the preacher cited the case of the woman who tried to touch the hem of the Saviour's garment as an instance of great faith.

"Remember," he said, "she did not seek to press the fabric, to retain it or even to seize it firmly. She knew that just a little touch would suffice. Just a little touch!"

"Not one drop," shouted the druggist, half awake, "unless you've got a prescription!"

* * *

A girl with a good figure, wavy hair, a smooth complexion and pretty teeth never has to worry about brains.

The Face On the Barroom Floor

What is the greatest poem in the English language?

Take as many guesses as you want—the chances are that whatever your literary taste, you're wrong.

Measured by requests for republication, the greatest poem is "The Face On the Barroom Floor."

Maybe it'll be different, now that the country has gone dry—or now that there isn't any barroom floor. Guessing that way, let's give the old favorite of thousands of serious and comic reciters a farewell appearance of this ditty.

By H. A. D'Arcy

'Twas a balmy summer evening, and a goodly crowd was there
Which well-nigh filled Joe's barroom, on the corner of the square;
And as songs and witty stories came through the open door,
A vagabond crept slowly in and posed upon the floor.

"Where did it come from " some one said. "The wind has blown it in."
"What does it want?" another cried. "Some whiskey, rum or gin?"
"Here, Toby, sic 'em, if your stomach's equal to the work—
I wouldn't touch him with a fork, he's filthy as a Turk."

This badinage the poor wretch took with stoical good grace;
In fact, he smiled as tho' he thought he'd struck the proper place.
"Come, boys, I know there's kindly hearts among so good a crowd—
To be in such good company would make a deacon proud.

"Give me a drink—that's what I want—I'm out of funds, you know.
When I had cash to treat the gang this hand was never slow.
What? You laugh as if you thought this pocket never held a sou;
I once was fixed as well, my boys, as any one of you.

"There, thanks, that's braced me nicely; God bless you one and all;
Next time I pass this good saloon I'll make another call.
Give you a song? No, I can't do that; my singing days are past;
My voice is cracked, my throat's worn out, and my lungs are going fast.

I'll tell you a funny story, and a fact, I promise, too.
"Say! Give me another whisky, and I tell you what I'll do—
That I was ever a decent man not one of you would think;
But I was, some four or five years back. Say, give me another drink.

"Fill her up, Joe, I want to put some life into my frame—
Such little drinks to a bum like me are miserably tame;
Five fingers—there, that's the scheme—and corking whisky, too.
Well, here's luck boys, and landlord, my best regards to you.

"You've treated me pretty kindly and I'd like to tell you how
I came to be the dirty sot you see before you now.
As I told you, once I was a man, with muscle, frame and health,
And but for a blunder ought to have made considerable wealth.

"I was a painter—not one that daubed on bricks and wood,
But an artist, and, for my age, was rated pretty good.
I worked hard at my canvas, and was bidding fair to rise,
For gradually I saw the star of fame before my eyes.

"I made a picture, perhaps you've seen, 'tis called the 'Chase of Fame,'
It brought me fifteen hundred pounds and added to my name,
And then I met a woman—now comes the funny part—
With eyes that petrified my brain, and sunk into my heart.

"Why don't you laugh? 'Tis funny that the vagabond you see
Could ever love a woman, and expect her love for me;
But 'twas so, and for a month or two her smiles were freely given,
And when her loving lips touched mine, it carried me to heaven.

"Boys, did you ever see a girl for whom your soul you'd give,
With a form like the Milo Venus, too beautiful to live;
With eyes that would beat the Koh-i-noor, and a wealth of chestnut hair?
If so, 'Twas she, for there never was another half so fair.

"I was working on a portrait, one afternoon in May,
Of a fair-haired boy, a friend of mine, who lived across the way;
And Madeline admired it, and, much to my surprise,
Said she'd like to know the man that had such dreamy eyes.

"It didn't take long to know him, and before the month had flown
My friend had stole my darling, and I was left alone;
And ere a year of misery had passed above my head,
The jewel I had treasured so had tarnished and was dead.

"That's why I took to drink, boys, Why, I never saw you smile.
I thought you'd be amused, and laughing all the while.
Why what's the matter, friend? There's a tear-drop in your eye.
Come, laugh like me; 'tis only babes and women that should cry.

"Say, boys, if you give me just another whisky I'll be glad,
And I'll draw right here a picture of the face that drove me mad.
Give me that piece of chalk with which you mark the baseball score—
You shall see the lovely Madeline upon the barroom floor."

Another drink, and with chalk in hand, the vagabond began
To sketch a face that well might buy the soul of any man.
Then, as he placed another lock upon the shapely head,
With a fearful shriek, he leaped and fell across the picture—dead.

* * *

She Should Know

For some hours the husband had sat in deep thought.

At last the wife speaks.

"What in the world is on your mind?"

"I have just been wondering," he explains. "Just wondering."

"Wondering? About what?"

"Well, no sooner were we married than you induced me to stop smoking, swearing and taking an occasional nip. Then you got me to stop reading light literature. Then you got me to throw away all the pictures I had accumulated in bachelor days. Then you had me go to a new tailor, and you bought my shirts and collars and ties yourself, so that they would not be the kind I had always worn. Then you made me grow a moustache and you made me have my hair cut differently. And one by one you weaned me away from my old friends and had me cultivate new ones. Also you stopped my regular custom of spending every other Sunday with some of my relatives until now I am on the merest speaking terms with my family. Also, through your suggestion, I have dropped cards, billiards and abandoned my usual fishing trips, cut out the football games, musical comedies and all that sort of thing. So I have just been wondering."

"Been wondering what, Harold?"

"Wondering, if I was so unsatisfactory in all these respects, what in the name of all that's human you found in me to love enough to marry me."

* * *

Romance Shattered

Mrs. Hemmandhaw—"I was disappointed this afternoon."

Hemmandhaw—"How?"

"Just as I came up behind two girls one of them was saying 'and he squeezed, and squeezed and squeezed—"

"Ah!"

"And while I was passing she said;

"'And squeezed and squeezed, but try as he might, he couldn't save a cent out of thirty dollars a week.'"

* * *

No Objection, It Seems

An elderly man of gouty tendency lived in dread of paralysis. When the fear came upon him he would pinch himself frantically to make sure that his enemy had not attacked him.

One night at a dinner party his worst fears were confirmed.

"Come at last! Come at last " he groaned. "Total insensibility of the right limb."

His partner alarmed, craved enlightenment. On being told the tragedy she said:

"Oh well, if it's any consolation to you, I may as well tell you that it was my leg you were pinching."

'Twould Be a Race

A lecturer was talking on the drink question.

"Now, supposing I had a pail of water and a pail of beer on this platform, and then brought on a donkey, which of the two would he take?"

"He'd take the water," came a voice from the gallery.

"And why would he take the water?" asked the lecturer.

"Because you would beat him to the beer," was the reply.

* * *

Rather Embarrassing

A young Californian often visited a leading Santa Barbara hotel because of its excellent honey.

When the young man got married, the wedding trip included this hotel, so that the bride might taste this ambrosial spread.

But the first morning there was no honey on the breakfast table. The bridegroom frowned. He called the old, familiar waiter.

"Where is my honey?" he demanded.

The waiter hesitated, looked awkwardly at the bride, then he stammered: "Er—er—Mamie don't work here no more, sir."

* * *

Mebbe

Let's be gay while we may
And seize love with laughter,
I'll be true as long as you,
And not a moment after.

The Harpy

By Robert W. Service.

From The Spell of the Yukon—By permission of the publishers of Service's Works, Barse & Hopkins, 21-39 Division Street, Newark, N. J.

There was a woman, and she was wise; woefully wise was she;
She was old, so old, yet her years all told were but a score and three;
And she knew by heart, from finish to start, the Book of Iniquity.

There is no hope for such as I on earth, nor yet in Heaven;
Unloved I live, unloved I die, unpittied, unforgiven;
A loathed jade, I ply my trade, unhallowed and unshriven.

I paint my cheeks, for they are white, and cheeks of chalk men hate;
Mine eyes with wine I make them shine, that men may seek and sate;
With overhead a lamp of red I sit me down and wait.

Until they come, the nightly scum, with drunken eyes aflame;
Your sweethearts, sons, ye scornful ones—'tis I who know their shame.
The gods, ye see, are brutes to me—and so I play my game.

For life is not the thing we thought, and not the thing we plan;
And Woman in a bitter world must do the best she can——
Must yield the stroke, and bear the yoke, and serve the will of man;
Must serve his need and ever feed the flame of his desire,
Though be she loved for love alone, or be she loved for hire;
For every man since life began is tainted with the mire.

And though you know he love you so and set you on love's throne;
You let your eyes but mock his sighs, and let your heart be stone,
Lest you be left (as I was left) tainted and alone.

From love's close kiss to hell's abyss is one sheer flight, I trow,
And wedding ring and bridal bell are will-o'-wisps of woe,
And 'tis not well to love too well, and this all women know.

Wherefore, the wolf-pack having gorged upon the lamb, their prey,
With siren smile and serpent guile I make the wolf-pack pay—
With velvet paws and clenching claws, a tigress roused to slay.

One who in youth sought truest truth and found a devil's lies;
A symbol of the sin of man, a human sacrifice.
Yet shall I blame on the man the shame? Could it be otherwise?

Was I not born to walk in scorn where others walk in pride?
The Maker marred, and, evil starred, I drift upon His tide;
And He alone shall judge His own, so I His judgment bide.

Fate has written a tragedy; its name is "The Human Heart."
The Theatre is the House of Life; Woman the mummer's part;
The Devil enters the prompter's box and the play is ready to start.

* * *

Sammy Was Some Mammy

Sambo was presented with a large cocoanut and as it was the first time he had ever seen a nut of this species, his curiosity got the best of him. He carried the nut to the village constable so as to find out what he really possessed. The constable was a practical joker and promptly informed Sambo that he was the proud possessor of a mule's egg. He further advised the darky to sleep with the "egg" every night and that soon he would hatch out a young mule.

Sambo was a faithful "mother" to the "egg" for two weeks. His patience finally was exhausted and one day he carried his prize to the outskirts of the village and heaved it into a nearby thicket. To his surprise and chagrin, a long-eared Texas jack-rabbit leaped into the air from the thicket and galloped away.

"Hey, you fool mule," yelled Sambo. "Come back here, don't yo know that I'se your mammy?"

* * *

Farmers' paper tells us that "Some ganders will mate with just one goose; some with two; some with three; and we have seen some with as many as six, but this is unusual." So that ganders are like a good many men!

Questions and Answers

Dear Whiz Bang Bill—I am soon to be married. What legal formalities are necessary?—***Goosey Gus.***

In these great and glorious days of jazz, a man about to be hooked-up should buy two licenses—one for a wife and the other for a car.

* * *

Dear Editor—Did you like Eleanor Glyn's Three Weeks?—***Irene Snappy.***

I don't know. I was ashamed to read it.

* * *

Dear Skipper—What is this? "Use me well and I am everybody, scratch my back and I am nobody."—***O. I. Sighe.***

A mirror.

* * *

Dear Captain Billy—The fellow I am engaged to has fallen in love with a bathing girl. What shall I do?—***Agnes.***

If you don't look well in a bathing suit, fall in love with a movie hero and then marry your fellow.

* * *

Dear Captain Billy—I had to walk home from an automobile trip. How can I avoid this?—***Jane.***

Bring a bicycle with you next time.

Dear Captain Billy—Why do people laugh in their sleeves?—***Goofey Gob.***

Now, there goes that "funny-bone" gag again.

* * *

Dear Bill—What's a "Weejee" board?—***Tiny Thomas.***

It's a piece of plank entirely surrounded by suckers.

* * *

Dear Captain Bill—My fiance says she will not marry me until I have done something big in life. Can you suggest something?—***Worried Romeo.***

Why not try washing elephants.

* * *

Dear Skipper—Please give me a definition of joy.—***Minnie Mumm.***

Joy is the peculiar feeling experienced by a man after a drunk when he counts his money and discovers that he has all the cash he thought he had and a few dollars more.

* * *

Dear Captain Billy—What do you think of a man who constantly deceives his wife?—***Kid M. Wright.***

I think he is a wonder.

* * *

Dear Capt. Billy—With Selma taking a hurried hike down Snoose Boulevard, how much shorter could she wear her skirts; how much lower could she wear her waist, and still hide her hide?—***Torkel Torkelson.***

I dunno.

Dear Capt. Billy—I feel so blue today. Last night I said something to my wife she didn't like and she hasn't spoken to me for a week. What can I do to regain her friendship?—***Blue Bill.***

Say, old timer, please tell me by return mail what it was you said to her.

* * *

Dear Captain Billy—What do you think is a literary man's happiest moment?—***James Whitcomb Riley Levinsky.***

When he has a long item in a woman's magazine under his own name.

* * *

Dear Billy—Can you compose a short sentence using every letter of the alphabet?—***Bill Klector.***

Pack my box with five dozen liquor jugs.

* * *

Dear Captain—Can you name some much-needed inventions?—***Bert Illion.***

Noiseless soup spoons, knives that will hold peas, muzzles for bed-bugs.

* * *

Dear Captain Bill—Why are women always going to bargain sales in hope of getting something for nothing?—***U. Kalaylee.***

For the same reason that men are always going to poker clubs.

* * *

Monsieur le Captain—What is the best way to make love?—***Rox Salt.***

The most stupid way possible; then the girl will believe you are in earnest.

Hoot Mon! Whusky!

WE HAVE it from no less a person than Bob Edwards, whom we believe is the author of the famous song, "The Sickly Souse of Saskatoon Squawks and Squeals in the Village Choir," that we are at last to have a real Scottish motion picture.

It has been a long time coming, but the scenario of a film depicting the affecting story of Auld Robin Gray, we gladly give it to our readers. The author must be a Scotchman himself, for he has everything down fine. It is, as we say, most affecting.

Characters:

Teenie
Jamie
Feyther
Mither
Auld Robin Gray

1. Closeup of Teenie and Jamie doing the sad farewell. Ship in the distance.

2. Teenie on shore, waving handkerchief and weeping. Ship moves slowly out of harbor.

3. Jamie in ship's rigging, looking sorrowfully to shore.

4. Teenie, bowed with grief, walking slowly through heather.

5. Feyther, Mither and Teenie in their lit-

tle home. Feyther goes to cupboard, takes out bottle. Drinks. Subtitle:

Feyther Maun Have His Drappie

6. Auld Robin Gray in his stillhouse in the heather, boiling up a mess of smoke. Barrels and bottles piled on every hand. Officer steps in. Robin hands him a bottle. Officer takes drink and departs with bottle. Robin registers resignation at loss.

7. Jamie on ship, slushing rigging.

8. Feyther, Mither and Teenie in cottage. Feyther goes to cupboard. Takes out bottle. Bottle empty. Registers horrified amazement. Subtitle:

"Hoot Mon! The Whusky's Gie Oot!"

9. Mither runs to Feyther's side. Examines bottle. Turns it upside down. Tries to shake out a drop. Nothing doing. Subtitle:

"The Whusky's Gie Oot!"

10. Feyther, Mither and Teenie, still in cottage. Feyther walks about pausing to bite a piece of the door jamb. Mither shakes her head despairingly. Teenie weeps.

11. Teenie crossing the heather—a jug in her hand.

12. Teenie enters Robins' still. Holds out her jug. Robin looks up. Subtitle:

"Wad Ye Gie Us Credit For a Little Whusky, Sir?"

13. Robin slacks the fire under the still. Rises and walks over to Teenie. Subtitle:

"Ha' Ye No Siller, Lass?"

14. Teenie sinks down before him. Weeps and shakes her head pathetically.

15. Robin lifts her tenderly and getting a bottle gives her a wee bit drappie. Tries to put his arms around her.

16. Teenie springs back and looks at him reprovingly.

17. Robin gazes at her keenly. Subtitle:

"Ye'd Mak an Auld Man a Gude Wife"

18. Teenie runs out of still. Next three pictures take her over the heather and into the cottage, jug in hand.

22. Feyther meets her eagerly. Takes the jug. Shows by its heft that it is empty. Makes as if to slam Teenie over the dome with it.

23. Jamie in America, digging for gold.

24. Teenie in cottage tells in pantomime what happened in the still.

25. Mither soothes her. Subtitle:

"Why Not? He's No So Auld"

26. Feyther takes Teenie by the shoulder and shakes her. Subtitle:

"An' He's Got Unleemited Whusky"

27. Teenie, Mither and Feyther in cottage. Feyther laboring with his thirst. Subtitle:

"Whusky! Whusky! Whusky!

28. Auld Robin Gray comes in with a full jug. Pours a little in a cup and tosses it off. Feyther watches him and tries to rise. Subtitle:

"Whusky! Whusky! Whusky!

29. Auld Robin looks at Teenie affectionately. Subtitle:

If I Gie Him a Drap Will Ye Gae Wi' Me to the Kirk?"

30. Closeup of Teenie, who is registering dismay.

31. Cut back to picture of Jamie and Teenie parting.

32. Feyther writhing on floor. Mither pleading in pantomime with Teenie.

33. Teenie turns to Robin. Subtitle:

"Aye, if I Maun, I Maun"

34. Teenie and Robin coming from kirk. Feyther following with a jug and a jag.

35. Jamie in America discovering gold and shoveling it into a sack.

36. Feyther, Mither, Robin and Teenie in cottage. Kegs and bottles piled on all the tables and chairs. Feyther, Mither and Robin with a pretty fair start, and hard at work at a loving cup, which Teenie, in tears, passes around.

37. Jamie, with his bag of gold, boards ship, homeward bound.

38. Jamie lands in Scotland.

39. Jamie reaches cottage door. Raps. No answer. Looks in through window.

40. Teenie starts back as if seeing an apparition.

41. Teenie goes to window and raises it.

42. Jamie tries to take her in his arms through window. She starts back. Subtitle:

"What's Wrang? I Bring Ye Gold"

4v. Teenie falls in a chair. Subtitle:

"Too Late, Jamie. I Married Auld Robin for His Whusky!"

44. Jamie leaps in through the window. Gazes on recumbent forms of Robin and Feyther. Sniffs at jugs and bottles. Pours himself a stiff drink and disposes of it. Subtitle:

" 'Twas Worth the Sacrifice, Lass. I Forgie Ye"

45. Jamie, his bag in one hand and a keg on his shoulders, goes over the heather back to the ship for America. Fade out. The end.

* * *

Camouflaged

He picked it up at a small garage,
And thought himself in clover
To buy a car so cheap—and found
'Twas his old one, painted over!

He picked her up at the fancy ball,
And proved a charming lover—
Then found, instead of a brand new girl,
'Twas his old one, painted over!

* * *

Hugh Hughes Hews and Hews

"There isn't much I don't know about the English language," boasted the long-haired man in the club. "I'll test you," a friend picked him up quickly. "I'll dictate a paragraph to you." With an assured air the boaster seized his pencil, but his jaw dropped as he heard: "As Hugh Hughes was hewing a yule log from a yew tree a man dressed in clothes of a dark hue came up to Hugh and said: 'Have you seen my ewes?' 'If you will wait until I hew this yew tree I will go with you anywhere in Europe to look for your ewes,' said Hugh."

Oh, Cholly, Let's Buy One, Too

I am thinking of getting one, whatcha say? I know it will feel funny at first and I know I'll never get used to wearing it, but some people think it helps a man's personal appearance equally as much as it does a lady's, so I have decided to try it. I do not intend to buckle mine around tight for that's unhealthy—prevents circulation, you know. I was accused of wearing one by a "jane" on the beach, last night. I know the boys will guy me for it looks so effeminate and sissy. It will be lots of trouble to get it on every morning because I must take it off before retiring. But I can get the bunch to help me. I want mine pretty large so I can have free movement of the muscles. Nearly every girl I've seen wears one and I intend to get one, too, for everybody says that there's nothing more useful than a wrist watch.

* * *

Coming and Going

Here are some of the reasons why girls leave home:

For bright lights.
For long moonlight rides.
For wonderful clothes.
For charge accounts at big stores.
For big town sweeties.

And why they come back:

To get a good rest.
To get married.
To eat wholesome ham and eggs.
To fool some sucker.

Rattlin' Joe's Prayer

By Captain Jack Crawford

Just pile on some o' them pine knots,
An' squat yoursel's down on this skin,
An' Scotty, let up on yer growlin'—
The boys are all tired o' yer chin.
Alleghany, jist pass round the bottle,
An' give the lads all a square drink,
An' as soon as yer settled I'll tell ye
A yarn as 'll please ye, I think.

'Twas the year eighteen hundred an' sixty,
A day in the bright month o' June,
When the Angel o' Death from the Diggin's
Snatched "Monte Bill"—known as McCune.
Wal, Bill was a favorite among us,
In spite o' the trade that he had,
Which war gamblin'; but—don't you forget it—
He of'n made weary hearts glad;
An', pards, while he lay in that coffin,
Which we hewed from the trunk o' a tree,
His face war as calm as an angel's,
An' white as an angel's could be.

An' thar's war the trouble commenced, pards,
Thar war no gospel-sharps in the camps,
An' Joe said: "We can't drop him this way,
Without some directions or stamps."
Then up spoke old Sandy McGregor,
"Look'ee yar, mates, I'm reg'lar dead stuck,
I can't hold no hand at religion,
An' I'm 'feared Bill's gone in out o' luck,
If I knowed a darn thing about prayin',
I'd chip in an' say him a mass;
But I ain't got no show in the layout,
I can't beat the game, so I pass."

Rattlin' Joe war the next o' the speakers,
An' Joe war a friend o' the dead;
The salt water stood in his peepers,
An' these are the words as he said:
"Mates, ye know as I ain't any Christian,
An' I'll gamble the good Lord don't know
That thar lives sich a rooster as I am;
But thar once war a time, long ago,

When I war a kid; I remember.
My old mother sent me to school,
To the little brown church every Sunday,
Whar they said I was dumb as a mule.
An' I reckon I've nearly forgotten

Purty much all thet ever I knew.
But still, if ye'll drop to my racket,
I'll show ye jist what I kin do.
"Jist hand me them cards off the rack;
"Now I'll show you my Bible," said Joseph—
"I'll convince ye thet this are a Bible,"
An' he went to work shufflin' the pack.
He spread out the cards on the table,
An' begun kinder pious-like: "Pards,
If ye'll jist cheese yer racket an' listen,
I'll show ye the pra'ar-book in cards.
"The 'ace,' that reminds us of one God,
The 'deuce,' of the Father an' Son,
The 'tray,' of the Father an' Son, Holy Ghost,
For, ye see, all them three are but one.
The 'four-spot,' is Matthew, Mark, Luke an' John,
The 'five-spot,' the virgins who trimmed
Their lamps while yet it was light of the day,
And the five foolish virgins who sinned.
The 'six-spot,'—in six days the Lord made the world,
The sea and the stars in the heaven;
He saw it war good w'at He made, then He said,
I'll jist go the rest on the 'seven.'
The 'eight-spot' is Noah, his wife an' three sons,
An' 'Noah's three sons had their wives;
God loved the hull mob, so bid em' emb-ark—
In the freshet He saved all their lives.
The nine war the lepers of biblical fame,
A repulsive an' hideous squad—
The 'ten' are the holy commandments, which came
To us perishin' creatures from God.
The 'queen' war of Sheba in old Bible times,
The 'king' represents old King Sol.
She brought in a hundred young folks, gals an' boys,
To the King in his government hall.
They were all dressed alike, an' she axed the old boy
(She put up his wisdom as bosh)
Which war boys an' which gals. Old Sol said: 'By Joe,
How dirty their hands! Make 'em wash!'
An' then he showed Sheba the boys only washed
Their hands and a part o' their wrists,
While the gals jist went up their elbows in suds.
Sheba weakened an' shook the king's fists.
Now, the 'knave,' that's the Devil, and, God, ef ye please,
Jist keep his hands off'n poor Bill.
An' now lads, jist drop on yer knees for a while
Till I draw, and perhaps I kin fill;
An' hevin' no Bible, I'll pray on the cards,
Fur I've showed ye they're all on the squar',
An' I think God 'll cotton to all that I say,
If I'm only sincere in the pra'r.

Jist give him a corner, good Lord—not on stocks,
Fur I ain't such a durned fool as that,
To ax ye fur anything worldly fur Bill,
Kase ye'd put me up then fur a flat.
I'm lost on the rules o' yer game, but I'll ax
Fur a seat fur him back o' the throne,
And I'll bet my hull stack thet the boy'll behave
If yer angels jist lets him alone.
Thar's nuthin' bad bout him unless he gets riled—
The boys'll all back me in that—
But if any one treads on his corns, then you bet
He'll fight at the drop o' the hat.
Jist don't let yer angels run over him, Lord,
Nor shut off all to once on his drink;
Break him in kinder gentle an' mild on the start,
An he'll give ye no trouble, I think.
An' couldn't ye give him a pack of old cards,
To amuse himself once in a while?
But I warn ye right hyar, not to bet on his game,
Or he'll get right away with yer pile.
An' now, Lord, I hope thet ye've tuck it all in,
An' listened to all thet I've said.
I know that my prayin' is jist a bit thin,
But I've done all I kin for the dead.
An' I hope I hain't troubled yer Lordship too much—
So I'll cheese it axin' again
Thet ye won't let the 'knave' get his grip on poor Bill.
Thet's all, Lord—your truly—Amen."

* * *

Vat Time Iss Idt?

Ikey said to Solomon. "Mine boy Israel is de smartest boy in town." Israel was four years old and his father said to him: "Issy, vat time is idt?"

"Four minutes to twelve, fadder," said Israel.

Ikey repeated the question and received the same answer.

"No, Issy, dot is wrong. It is five minutes to twelfe."

"I knew it all de time," said Issy, "but I knew you vould chew me down so I said four."

Beating the Biscuit Shooter!

A timid looking little man took a seat at the counter of a railroad eating house and ordered ham and eggs. He looked bewildered when the waiter turned his face toward the kitchen and yelled, "a mogul with two headlights."

A second later the man said, "Beg pardon, sir, I'd like to have those eggs turned over." "Blanket the headlights," yelled the waiter.

An engineer took his seat at the counter. "Wheat cakes and coffee for mine," he said. "Running orders," yelped the waiter, briskly.

"A beefsteak, well done," said the last arrival. "A hot box and have it smoking," was the information given the cook.

"Some scrambled eggs, please," piped an old lady with trepidation. The waiter turned around and yelled, "Wreck 'em on the main line."

A boomer brakeman noisily set down his lamp, and mounted one of the stools. "Let's see your price list," he commanded.

"Gimmie a couple of battleships, and a pan of Murphy's on the main line, and a string of flats on the siding," he ordered. It was the waiter's turn to look mystified. "Cut the cow-car off the java train," continued the boomer, "and switch me a couple of life preservers for a consolidation, and as its a long drag to the next feed tank, you better fill the auxiliary to its full capacity."

"Say," interrupted the biscuit shooter, "I've

only been here a week, and you left me at the first stop!"

"Excuse me," apologized the boomer, "I thought you were an old head. Gimmie a couple of porkchops, and some fried potatoes, and a side order of wheat cakes. Then for the second course, you can bring me some black coffee, and some doughnuts. Fill the lunch bucket, too, because it's a long drag to the next feed factory. Put the coffee in the top, and fill the bottom deck with sandwiches and pie."

"I got you, Steve," replied the waiter.

* * *

The Dying Hobo

'Twas dawn by a western water tank,
One cold November day;
There in an open boxcar,
A dying hobo lay.

His partner stood beside him,
With a sadly drooping head,
Listening to the last words
That the dying hobo said.

Good-by ld pal, I'm going
To a l d where all is bright,
Where handouts grow in the bushes ,
And you can sleep out every night.

The dying hobo's head dropped back,
As he sang his last refrain,
His partner stole his shoes and socks
And grabbed an eastbound train.

* * *

Ever Tried It?

"What is it when you're married twice at the same time?"

"Polygamy."

"And when you're only married once?"

"Monotony."

A Pathetic Tragedy

HER sweetheart invited her to go to a cabaret with him and she wanted to look her very best.

After her perfumed bath she lay down on the couch and relaxed for a half hour.

Then she drew on her silk hose and her slippers, which were very high of heel and very pointed of toe.

She massaged her face with cold cream, powdered it lightly, touched her lips, chin and cheeks with rouge, then powdered again.

Her eyebrows were already shaven to the regulation thin line and she darkened them a little with an eyebrow pencil.

She touched her eyelashes to make them look longer.

She puffed her hair over her ears and coiled it low in the back.

She manicured her nails and rubbed cold cream into her elbows.

Her skirt was very long and her waist was very low. Her hat and wrap were of the latest design.

She sat down in front of the mirror and practiced bringing and holding a sweet expression.

But when she finally arrived she felt dreadfully undressed.

She had forgotten her bead chain, and every lady there had some sort of beads around her neck.

* * *

A Matter of Diet

A negro employed at one of the movie studios in Los Angeles was drafted by a director to do a novel comedy scene with a lion.

"You get into this bed," ordered the director, "and we'll bring the lion in and put him in bed with you. It will be a scream."

"Put a lion in bed with me!" yelled the negro. "No, sah! Not a-tall! I quits right here and now."

"But," protested the director, "this lion won't hurt you. This lion was brought up on milk."

"So was I brung up on milk," wailed the negro, "but I eats meat now."

* * *

Tips on the Ponies

"Carpet"—Should be hard to beat.
"My Friend Wife"—Sure to be heard from.
"Fawcett"—Should run well.
"Patient"—Will improve.
"Leopard"—Runs well in spots.
"Money"—May last long enough.
"Rubber"—Tires in the stretch.
"Yawn"—Can close a gap.
"Flivver"—Speedy, but stops occasionally.
"Fly-wheel"—Has a good turn occasionally.

The Suicide

I am standing on the threshold of eternity at last,
As reckless of the future as I have been of the past,
I am void of all ambition, I am dead to every hope;
The coil of life has ended, I am letting go the rope.

I have drifted down the stream of life till weary, sore oppressed,
And I'm tired of the motion, and simply want a rest.
I have tasted all the pleasures that life can hold for man,
I've scanned the whole world over till there's nothing left to scan.

I have heard the finest music, I have read the rarest books,
I have drunk the purest vintage and tasted all the cooks,
I have run the scale of living and sounded every tone,
So there is nothing left to live for and I long to be alone.

Alone and unmolested where the vultures do not rave;
And the only refuge left me is the placid, quiet grave;
I am judge and jury mingled and the verdict that I give
Is, that minus friends and money it is foolishness to live.

In a day or two my body will be found out in the lake;
The coroner will get a fee, the printer get a "take";
The usual verdict, "Suicide from causes yet unknown."
And Golgotha draws another blank—a mound without a stone.

To change the usual verdict I will give the reason now,
Before the rigid seal of death is stamped upon my brow;
'Tis the old familiar story of passion, love and crime,
Repeated through the ages since Cleopatra's time.

A woman's lips, a woman's eyes—a siren all in all;
A modern Circe, fit to cause the strongest man to fall;
A wedded life, some blissful years, and poverty drops in
With care and doubt and liquor from whiskey down to gin.

The story told by Tolstoi in comparison with mine
Is moonlight unto sunlight, as water unto wine;
The jealous pangs I suffered, the hideous nights of woe,
I pray no other mortal may ever undergo.

But I've said enough I fancy, to make the reasons plain—
Enough to show the causes of a shattered heart and brain.
What wonder, then, that life holds not a single thread to bind
A wish or hope to live for, an interest in mankind.

Already dead, but breathing—a fact that I regret—
A man without desire, excepting to forget;
And, since there is denied me one, why should I linger here,
A dead leaf from the forest of a long-forgotten year?

So, au revoir, old cronies: If there's a meeting place beyond,
I'll let you know in spirit and I know you will respond;
I'm going now, old comrades, to heaven or to hell;
I'll let you know which shortly; Farewell, a long farewell.

* * *

A Friendly Household

"A flirt, am I?" exclaimed Mary Ann, under notice to go. "Well, I knows them as flirts more than I do, and with less excuse." She shot a spiteful look at her mistress, and added, "I'm better looking than you. More handsome. 'Ow do I know? Your husband told me so."

"That will do," said her mistress frigidly.

"But I ain't finished yet!" retorted Mary Ann. "I can give a better kiss than you! Want to know who told me that, ma'am?"

"If you mean to suggset that my husband—"

"No, it wasn't your husband this time," said Mary Ann. "It was your chauffeur."

* * *

Lovely Lieuts.

"Why do the Smiths put on so many airs these days?"

"They got that way by having a second lieutenant in the family."

"I see."

"And despite the fact that he has been mustered out and has resumed his job as chambermaid in a livery stable, they can't forget how he looked in his uniform."

* * *

In a Pullman: "Colonel, shall I brush you off, suh?" asked the porter.

"No," returned the colonel, "I'll get off in the usual way."

'Tis Terrible!

"You led me on! You received my advances! I lied for you; stole, fought and slew for you! Not a day passed when I did not risk my honor, my very existence, for you and your cruel wishes. Miserable fool that I was, just to win your love I wrecked my life—wrecked it so surely as to make me a debauched, hated and outlawed man. Like a wretched slave my years were spent in carrying out your murderous, thieving, lying missions and whims. Twice I went on trial to save you, the perpetrator; twice I spent thousands to secure my freedom. In all the world was there mortal who suffered and endured for you, as I have suffered and endured for you, base woman? You tortured and haunted me; those saintly yet satanic eyes were always with me, ahead of me, blinding me; the eyes that proved my happiness and then my ruin. I loved you, heart and soul. My very existence was wrapped up in you. I believed in you as only a mother has faith in her boy. And you cheated me; defamed me; killed—"

Algernon could not go on.

"You read the rest, Marion, dear," he said, "it affects me so!"

Gone Are the Days

Want an eye-opener? * * * Have another * * * Skoll * * * This is on me * * * You know what the governor of North Carolina said to the governor of South Carolina? * * * A dash of bitters, please * * * Set 'em up again * * * Something soft on the side * * * Here's mud in your eye * * * Let's make a night of it * * * I knew a guy in Kentucky what died with a glass in his hand * * * Gimme a horse's neck * * * I wanta scuttle of suds with the foam on the bottom * * * A boilermaker and helper for me * * * Let's make it a nightcap * * * Good morning, Mr. Bartender * * * Good morning, hell, it's whisky you want * * * Nope, bromo seltzer * * * Gee! what a head!

* * *

The Road to Kissland

That Perkins' boy is awfully slow,
Parley vou.
That Perkins' boy is awfully slow,
Parley vou.
That Perkins' boy is awfully slow,
He believes me when I tell him "no."
Hinkey dinkey parley vou.

* * *

Those Dreadful Drummers

Four or five jolly drummers gathered in the smoking compartment of a Pullman car, and soon their conversation drifted to the great problem of the day—women. In the party also was a frock-coated pastor of serious mien.

The salesmen winked at each other as the minister entered, and then, as if to have some harmless pleasure, one after another started telling of the wonderful virtues of the knights of the grip.

"I am often away from home for four weeks at a time," one salesman commenced, "and I never even look at another woman."

"And I am so bound up in the charms of my wife that I'm ashamed to tip the check girls," declared the next one.

"Why, my wife is so good to me that I won't allow a woman to wait on me in a resaurant," said another.

Their conversation sounded too much like unadulterated bunk for the good minister to swallow, and he joined the party by offering a silk hat to any salesman present who could truthfully say he had always been faithful to his wife. The pastor won his point and the conversation soon drifted to other subjects.

The next day one of the salesmen arrived home and soon told his wife of the jolly party in the Pullman smoker.

"But, John," she said, "why didn't you take him up?" John's active salesman brain worked quickly.

"Why, Mable, you know I look like hell in a silk hat."

* * *

"I take a great interest in women's movements," said the earnest young reformer in the railway compartment.

The eyes of the weary-looking man with the dyed moustache and the baggy cheeks, lit up.

"Do you know of any new ones, laddie?" he whispered, hoarsely.

He Was Certainly Justified

According to the last issue of the San Antonio Harpoon, a negro was arrested in that city, charged with simple assault upon another colored gentleman. The counsel for the defense put the accused on the stand and instructed him to tell the jury about the fight.

"We wuz playin' seben-up, Boss," he began, addressing the audience in the court house, which he had mistaken for the jury, "fo' five dollars uh game. I had three, and de other niggah had four! It wuz my time to deal, an' I dealt 'im a han' and m'self uh han! He look at 'is han', an' I ax 'im what he's doin'. He says, 'Ise uh beggin'.' I den look at muh han', an' I had de deuce ob trumps, de ten spot ob trumps, an' de queen ob trumps. On dis han' I gib 'im one, makin' 'im five to muh three. He led de eight spot ob trumps, an' I gib 'im muh deuce. He nex' led de king ob trumps, an' I gib 'im muh ten spot. He nex' led de ace ob trumps—an' dens when I hit 'im."

The jury acquitted him, for no man in Bexar County can stand idly by and see the rules of an old-time game wantonly destroyed.

* * *

Rave On, McDuff

One dismal day when the wind blew high;
It made her fairly moan,
For everyone could plainly see—
She loved to roll her own.

* * *

"Three balls!" yelled the umpire. "Now's your chance to soak it," shouted the excited pawnbroker's clerk to the batsman.

In Old Missouri

A theatre in "one night" towns is always called by the natives, the "Opery House," and is usually up one or more flights of stairs, the stage furnished with dim lights, and the dressing room with nothing. In one of these "opery houses" in southwestern Missouri a certain theatrical manager found but one dressing room—a large apartment beneath the stage.

"Where are the other dressing rooms?" he wanted to know.

"There ain't any others," returned the local impresario.

"Well, what are we going to do? I have a large company of ladies and gentlemen, and they cannot dress in this one room."

"What's the matter?" drawled the Missourian. "Ain't they speakin'?"

* * *

Oh, Pickle My Bones

There had been a big reduction in forces on one of the principal eastern railroads and during this reduction the president of the railroad in question died. Everything was quiet at the home of the former president when the lid of the coffin which held him was lifted and he peered out and asked, "How many pallbearers have I?"

One of them who was standing nearby was dumbfounded but finally managed to say "Ten."

The former president promptly replied, "Cut off four."

* * *

A jug of brew; some jazz and—who?

The Uncomplaining Hot Dog

Customer—Are your wienies healthy?

Vender—I have never heard one complain of being sick.

* * *

Wifey wrote to Hubby, on a business trip, thusly:

Dear Bill: Please send me some money.

He replied: I haven't any money. Enclosed find check for 10,000 kisses.

Three days later he received the following:

Dear Bill: Received your check for 10,000 kisses. Many thanks. The Iceman cashed it.

—Your loving wife--------

* * *

St. Chrys No Piker

St. Chrysotom of the fourth century had his ideas on prohibition which are worth repeating, whether you agree with them or not. Said he:

I hear men cry when these deplorable excesses happen: "Would to God there was no wine!" What folly, what madness! When other men sin, you find fault with the gifts of God; What insanity in this? Is it the wine that causes this abuse? No, it is not the wine, but the intemperance of those who take an evil delight in it. But rather cry out: "Would to God that there were no drunkenness, no luxury!" But if you shout, "Would there were no wine!" you should add, would there were no iron because of the murders; would there were no night because of the thieves; would there were no light because of the informers; would there were no women on account of adulteries! In this way you might destroy everything; this is a devilish way of reasoning!

We showed the above to a couple of friends. One remarked, "Quite so, quite so, but St. Chrysotom wasn't acquainted with Scotch."

"Nor Bourbon," added another.

But Chrys. was all right, they both agreed.

Heard at the Club

Anne M. Burrows

Glad I caught you old scout—for I'm going away,
  And I wanted to say farewell;
I'm leaving New York at the break of day,
  For the land that the world calls hell.

The wife? Well, hardly, you see, pal mine,
  The lady who bears my name
Has squandered my guilders and drunk my wine,
  But never has played the game.

I've given her all, and she's given me naught,
  Though I've seated her on a throne;
The taste of love's bread I've so long forgot
  That I've ceased to ask for the stone.

She always was lavish enough with her smile,
  And with favors for others to glean;
But she's never considered me even worth while,
  Except as a money machine.

So I've found me a woman at last—a mate—
  A girl from the dark side of town;
But she's sick of it, too—and it's not too late,
  Though we both were sinking down.

We're going away to a brand new land,
  And we're going to start brand new.
The world may look on us both as damned,
  But we'll lift ourselves nearer the blue.

Just a bit nearer, believe me, old man,
  Than I've ever dared dream to be;
And I somehow don't think the good God can
  Judge harshly my love and me.

For I tell you He knows—God, yes, He knows,
  How hard I have struggled and worked,
And He sees, and He pities, and don't you suppose
  He can tell you the one who shirked?

So good-bye to the street, and the stress and the strain,
  Farewell to the social sham.
Adieu to this battle for gold and gain
  That breaks down the heart of a man.

I'm willing to take the full brunt of the blame;
  But I want you to understand—
The girl? Well, she's worth every bit of the game,
  God bless you, old boy, for your hand.

A Yiddish Knight

Knights of Columbus deny a story that has been going the rounds concerning "Mike Murphy." There is nothing to it.

It is said that one of their organizers dropped into a clothing store which had the name of "Mike Murphy" over the door. There was not a soul in the store at the time, so the organizer, being an original cuss, left an application on the counter with this note:

"Dear Mike: Fill out the blank and shoot 'er in. We want you."

It is said that the application was filled out, mailed to the organizer, and "Mike Murphy" elected to membership and initiated.

After the initiation a motion was made that the lodge give a banquet for the new class. "Mike" took the floor in a maiden speech to the Knights—and for the first time is was discovered that he was a Jew!

He was strong for the "bank-vit." It was so ordered.

Someone then moved that nothing but ham, pork and pigs' knuckles be served at the banquet, and that any member who failed to attend and partake of the feast was to be suspended without further ceremony.

"Mister Bresident," Mike cried as he jumped to his feet. "It isn't right you should have such a motion. You know I can't eat dot ham und odder pig meat what you are gonna have. If I don't attend, you will fire me out; und if I do attend and don't eat de meat, you will fire me anyhow. Vat kind of mongey-bizness you t'ink dis is? Now just to show you what's what I stend on my gonstitutional rights to amend any motion made. I moof you, derefore, Mister Bresident, that we have the banquet on Friday night."

* * *

To Helen Bach

Here's a Ford story you haven't heard, which may have some bearing on the "Forward Movement":

It happened in a church. The pastor had taken for the topic for his sermon, "Better Church Attendance."

The pastor held that the automobile had taken more people away from church than any other thing. He concluded with the explanation: "The Ford car has taken more people to hell than any other thing that I can mention!" Whereupon an old lady in the congregation began to clap her hands and moan: "Praise the Lord! Oh, Praise the Lord!"

"What's the matter, sister?" asked the pastor.

"The Ford never went any place that it couldn't make the round trip," she answered, "and I am sure that all those unfortunate people in hell will be back. Praise the Lord! Hallelujah!"

* * *

Suggested marriage service: To have and to scold; in sickness or wealth; for better or purse.

Everybody Gets Tagged

Man comes into this world naked and with nothing on him, but in a short time everybody has something on him.—Temple Topics.

* * *

He was to take her for a trip in his new yacht the next day, and she was questioning him about it.

"How awfully nice of you to name the boat after me," she giggled. "What is she like?"

"Well—er,' 'he answered—"she's not much to look at, don't ye know, but she's very fast."

* * *

Impossible

Scene: G. N. Depot at Minneapolis, Minn.

Man staggers into waiting room and clings to a pillar.

Elderly woman remarks excitedly: "Call the ambulance; he's terribly sick."

Her husband: "He's not sick; he's only drunk."

Elderly woman: "Why, how can that be possible since the country went dry?"

Grand finale: Sick man totters to the rest-room for another little bracer.

* * *

The Underworld

BY CLEM YORE

I want to be square to the underworld,
And even a dog that is down.
I'd rather be a painter of smiles
Than to carve a grewsome frown.
So sit you down by my bungalow
And we will enjoy the sky,
For brothers and sisters, pals of woe,
You're just as immortal as I.

Shifting the Responsibility

An Irish priest of our acquaintance told us the following little story as an exemplification of the difficulty of getting home a well-merited rebuke to his quick-witted race:

He was accustomed to go to the village barber's—one of his flock—for his daily shave. This man habitually drank more than he should and consequently in the morning his hand was not always steady. One day he cut the priest's chin, who thereupon said, with some severity: "Ah, Mick, 'tis the drink is the terrible thing."

"Thrue, your riverence," came the instant response, "it do make the skin so tinder."

* * *

Shall We Forgive Her?

"What party do you affiliate with?" asked the register of elections to a colored suffragette.

Astonished, she said: "Ah reckon ah don' want to vote if ah gotta tell de pahty's name, fo' he's one o' fines' gem'man in dis city."

* * *

Light and Dark Shades

A young colored couple were sitting at the foot of the Statue of Liberty. Henry was holding Mandy's hand.

"Henry," said Mandy, "does you-all know why dey has such small little lights on the Statue o' Liberty?"

"Ah dunno," replied the Ethiopian swain, "unless it's because de less light, de mo' liberty!"

Limber Kicks

Tabasco

One swallow does not make a summer,
Is good for poets to tell,
But I took one that was a hummer,
And going down, 'twas hotezell.

* * *

The Darkies' Triangle

Oh, Lookee hea' woman, look what you gone and done.
Made me love you sweetly, then your papa come.
Go way from hea', don' you knock on my door;
Sweet daddy come home, I can't have you no more.
You can call the blues, anything you please;
But the blues ain't nothin', but the heart disease.

* * *

.."You've got to admit,"
Chirped a geezer called Paige
"A girl on the knee
Is worth two on the stage."

* * *

Warm Toast

I'm awfully glad I met you,
And since I met you
I rather like you,
And since I like you
I think, I'll let you—be my Pal.

* * *

Just for old time's sake, let's sing that plaintive melody:

"At the bar, at the bar,
Where I smoked my first cigar,
And the nickels and the dimes rolled away;
It was only by chance
That I had them in my pants,
And now I am happy every day."

Uncle runs a freight train,
Brother runs a hack,
Father's making moonshine,
While sister balls-the-jack.

* * *

Our Pets

Call her duckie, if you please,
And she blushes and she sighs;
Say she's "chic" and straightway she's
Wafted into sunny skies.
Call her Birdie and she's glad;
Call her Chicken and she's gay—
Say she's just a hen, and then
Something warm will be to pay!

* * *

Motor Goose

Ride a cock horse to a town by the river,
To see an old lady driving a flivver;
She steers with her fingers and stops with her toes,
The noise wakes the neighbors wherever she goes.

* * *

The boy stood on the burning deck,
But he couldn't feel it burn;
He'd spent "Three Weeks" with Eleanor Glyn
On the banks of Lake Lucerne.

* * *

Oh! Bevo, Where Is Thy Sting?

Here's to a long life, and a merry one;
A quick death, and a painless one;
A pretty girl, and a loving one;
A cold bottle, and another one!

* * *

There was a young lady from Natchez,
Who fell in some nettleweed patches,
With a heart full of gloom
She sits in her room,
And scratches, and scratches and scratches.

* * *

Ring On, Oh Chimes!

I stood on the banks of a brook,
My senses were almost reeling,
Every once in a while I ventured a look,
For the village bells were peeling.

The Booze Fighter's Dream

I dreamed that I dwelt on an isle of cracked ice,
In the midst of a lake of champagne,
Where bloomed the mint juleps in meadows of green
Amid showers of lithia rain.

I reclined on a divan of lager beer foam,
With a pillow of froth for my head,
While a spray from a fountain of sparkling gin fizz,
Descended like dew on my head.

From far away mountains of crystalline ice
A zephyr refreshing and cool,
Came wafting the incense of sweet muscatel,
That sparkled in many a pool.

My senses were soothed by the soft purling song,
From a brooklet of pousee cafe,
That rippled along o'er pebbles of snow
To a river of absinthe frappe.

Then, lulled by the music of tinkling glass
From schooners that danced on the deep,
I dreamingly sipped up a high ball or two,
And languidly floated to sleep.

And then I awoke on a bed full of rocks,
With a bolster as hard as a brick,
A wrench in my neck, a rack in my head,
And a stomach detestibly sick.

With sand in my eyes, and grit in my throat,
Where the taste of last evening still hung,
And I felt that a bath towel was stuffed in my throat
Which I afterwards found was my tongue.

I groped for the thread of the evening before,
In the mystified maze of my brain,
Until a great light burst on me once more,
I'M OFF THE WAGON AGAIN!

* * *

Some Good Advice

The Young Thing—What kind of husband would you advise me to look out for?

Well-Meaning Friend—You let husbands alone, my dear—it's asking for trouble—you get a single man!

The Higher Education

"Now that we're engaged you must be quite frank and tell me everything."

"Yes, dearest. But there are some things that I don't know yet."

* * *

Snuff This, Snooser

I would if I could if I couldn't, how could I? I couldn't without I could, could you without you could. I couldn't, could you?

* * *

Hairoil's Advice

"I think I had better get a job before we marry."

"Don't be so unromantic, Harold, I won't need any clothes for a long, long time."

"But you may want to eat almost immediately, my dear."

* * *

Because a woman shuts her eyes when she is kissed it doesn't follow that she dare not meet the kiss face to face.

* * *

Perfume and Sich

Two salesgirls in a department store were discussing life in general. "What do you suppose is the matter with me anyway? I'm just sick of livin'," said one. Said the other: "I am, too. Take it from me, we need something aesthetic in our lives." "For Pete's sake, what is that?" "Aesthetic?" Why, you poor fish, it's putting perfume in your bath water, and things like that."

A Mean Car Company

Sandy was indignant because a certain street car company reduced its fare from 6c to 5c and wrote a letter to the company about it.

"For the past eight years I have been walking," Sandy wrote, "and thus saving $3.60 per month, whereas now I can only save $3.00 per month."

* * *

Her Rates

A colored woman applied to a lady for a job.

"What do you charge a day?" asked the mistress.

"Well, mum," was the reply, "a dollar and a quarter if I eats myself and a dollar if you eats me."

* * *

Is your husband a sound sleeper?

Yes, and the sound keeps me awake.

* * *

"How Dry I Am"

At a charge of American troops in the Argonne, the captain suddenly cried out, "Lie down!" as a hail of German bullets from a machine gun came over them. They all dropped but one.

"Great Scott, man, lie down!" shouted the officer.

The soldier tapped his hip pocket and called back in an explanatory way: "I can't. I've got a bottle of cognac in here and it hasn't any cork in it."

Benny Cleveland's Job

Benny Cleveland, in the days of the whaling industry, was a character in Nantucket, who advertised, when storms raged and husbands were absent at sea, that he "would sleep at the home of timid ladies for 15 cents a night, or two nights for a quarter." Joseph A. Campbell wrote the poem.

When portents are abroad at night and tempests lash the shore,
And mateless wives grow timid at the ocean's fearful roar,
'Tis then a gloom comes o'er me, and, with many a plaintive sob,
I long for quaint Nantucket and for Benny Cleveland's job.

In days of old brave knights were wont to guard the ladies fair,
Or rescue lovely maidens from the robber baron's lair;
But on no such quest chivalric was our Benny forced to roam—
He kept his knightly vigil each night at some dame's home.

His fee as Guardian Angel all Nantucketers well knew,
'Twas 15 cents for one night, or 25 for two;
So, trustful in his watchfulness, wives gave themselves to sleep,
To dream of absent husbands in their journeys o'er the deep.

* * *

Blood vs. Hootch

A Scotchman has been presented with a pint flask of rare old Scotch whisky. He was walking briskly along the road toward home, when along came a Ford which he did not sidestep in time. It threw him down and hurt his leg quite badly. He got up and limped down the road. Suddenly he noticed that something warm was trickling down his leg.

"Oh, God," be groaned, "I hope that's blood."

* * *

Sweetheart Blues

I got a man,
Won't tell you his name,
Cause your man
And my man
May be the same.

* * *

Our Original Song Success

The only rings I ever gave her were the rings beneath her eyes.

Give Us Banana 812?

A young West Indian negro recently arrived in New York City and was having his first experience in talking over the telephone. He was calling a relative of his, who was a domestic in a wealthy family, with a view of apprizing her of his presence in America. His sister, who was his instructor, was patiently explaining to him how to operate the instrument. The number he was to call was Riverside 1101.

The conversation was as follows:

"Hullo! I say, Hullo!"

West Indian—"Dis is Sam talking to you from the West Indies. I just arrived yesterday."

Operator—"Number, please."

"Do you hear me?"

"Operator—"Number, please; number, please."

"Can you see me?"

Operator—"Number, please. What number do you want?"

"I want to talk to my sister. She don't know I'm here and I don't want her to know it."

"What number do you want?"

"I want one, I want another one, I don't want nothing, and I want another one. Then you can give me Riverside."

The sister who became disgusted with his ignorance yanked the telephone out of his hand, pushed him out of the way and got Riverside 1101.

* * *

A trip on the ocean will bring out all the good that's in you.

How to Kiss Deliciously

THE gentleman must be taller than the lady he intends to kiss. Take her right hand in yours and draw her gently to you; pass your left hand over her right shoulder, diagonally down across her back, under her left arm, press her to your bosom; at the same time she will throw her head back, and you have nothing to do but lean a little forward and press your lips to hers, and then the thing is done.

Don't make a noise over it as if you were shooting craps, nor pounce down upon it like a hungry hawk upon an innocent dove; but gently fold the damsel in your arms, and by a sweet pressure upon her mouth revel in the blissfulness of your situation, without smacking your lips upon it is you would after imbibing the Bacchanalian draught, but like Venus sipping honey from the lips of—O! Shoo Fly!

* * *

She Knew

Teacher—Maisie, can you tell me the meaning of the word repentant?

Maisie—Yes, teacher. It's what a girl feels when she gets caught.

* * *

Oh, aspirin, dear aspirin, my head aches for you.

The Gila Monster Route

By Post and Norton.

The lingering sunset across the plain
Kissed the rear-end of an east-bound train,
And shone on a passing track close by,
Where a dingbat sat on a rotten tie.

He was ditched by a shack and a cruel fate,
The con highballed, and the manifest freight,
Pulled out on the stem behind the mail,
And she hit the ball on a sanded rail.

As she pulled away in the falling night,
He could see the gleam of her red tail-light,
Then the moon arose and the stars came out—
He was ditched on the Gila Monster Route.

Nothing in sight but sand and space;
No chance for a gink to feed his face,
Not even a shack to beg for a lump,
Or a henhouse to frisk for a single gump.

As he gazed far out on the solitude,
He drooped his head and began to brood,
He thought of the time he lost his mate,
In a hostile burg on the Nickel Plate.

They had mooched the stem and threw their feet,
And speared four-bits on which to eat,
And deprived themselves of their daily bread
And sluffed their coin for "Dago Red."

Down by the track in the jungle's glade,
On the cool green grass, in the tules shade,
They shed their coats and ditched their shoes,
And tanked up full of that colored booze.

Then they took a flop with their skins plumb full,
And they did not hear the harness bull,
Till he shook them out of their boozy nap,
With a husky voice and loaded sap.

They were charged with "vag" for they had no kale,
And the judge said, "Sixty days in jail."
But the John had a "bindle"—a worker's plea—
So they gave him a floater and set him free.

They had turned him up, but ditched his mate,
So he grabbed the guts of an east-bound freight,
He slung his form on a rusty rod,
Till he heard the shack say, "Hit the sod!"

The John piled off, he was in the ditch,
With two switch lamps and a rusty switch,
A poor old seedy, half starved bo,
On a hostile pike, without a show.

From away off somewhere in the dark,
Came the sharp, short note of a coyote's bark,
The bo looked 'round and quickly rose,
And shook the dust from his thread-bare clothes.

Off in the west through the moonlit night,
He saw the gleam of a big headlight—
An east-bound stock train hummed the rail;
She was due at the switch to clear the mail.

As she drew up close, the head end shack
Threw the switch to the passing track,
The stock rolled in and off the main,
And the line was clear for the west-bound train.

When she hove in sight far up the track,
She was working steam, with her brake-shoes slack,
She hollered once at the whistle post,
Then she flitted by like a frightened ghost.

He could hear the roar of the big six wheel,
And her drivers pound on the polished steel,
And the screech of her flanges on the rail,
As she beat it west o'er the desert trail.

Then John got busy and took a risk,
He climbed aboard and began to frisk,
He reached up high and began to feel
For the end-door pin—then he cracked the seal.

'Twas a double decked stock car filled with sheep—
Old John crawled in and went to sleep,
She whistled twice and highballed out,
They were off—down the Gila Monster Route.

* * *

The Housing Problem

The Gentleman—"Yes, he's a good little dog, but our rooms are so small, y'know; haven't you got a dog that wags his tail up and down?"

* * *

Women and music should never be dated.

Combinations

"I simply can't understand the combination of my wife's clothes."

"What puzzles you?"

"Well, when she wants to hide anything she pokes it down her neck, but when she wants to get at it again, it's always in her stocking."

* * *

A New Movement

"Look here man!. Doan yo' try none o' dat shimmy stuff wid me."

"Dat ain't shimmy, chile! Dat's fever an' ague!"

* * *

Volunteers

"Watch your step, Miss," cautioned the conductor.

"It isn't necessary," snapped the incoming passenger. "Those sapheads on the curb are doing it for me."

* * *

He Reads Whiz Bang, Maybe

A salesmanager complained to one of his salesmen, "Why is it that your traveling expenses always run above that of every other man on our force?"

The salesman wired back, "I'll bite, why is it?"

* * *

A Desk Motto

Youth carries swaggeringly that most dangerous of all blunderbusses, knowledge at half-cock.

Spring Fads

Tailors in convention assembled say that Spring styles will be looser and more comfortable. Little change in the trousers—as usual.

* * *

A Hop Fiend's Dream

A hop fiend out for a weary stroll,
Looking for a sucker that he might roll,
He hadn't smoked for the livelong day,
He was barred from the joint where he couldn't pay,
Down in Mexico where they go to blow.

He wanted a smoke and he wanted it bad,
Then he met a friend who money had;
He touched him quick and away he flew
To cop the dope from the Chink's bamboo,
Down in Mexico where they go to blow.

He smoked and he smoked and he smoked away,
Thinking of the riches that he'd have next day;
He had a million horses, cattle and sheep,
And a thousand ships that sailed the deep,
Down in Mexico where they go to blow.

He had a thousand ladies and all were fair,
With dreamy blue eyes and golden hair,
Some were short and some were tall,
But he said, "By gad, I'll love 'em all,"
Down in Mexico where they go to blow.

He had a thousand dollars in nickels and dimes,
And he counted them over 'bout a thousand times,
Then he stabbed himself with a yen-shee-gow,
And he died with his head on a suey-bow,
Down in Mexico where they go to blow.

* * *

We'll Vouch For This

What are little girls made of, made of?
What are little girls made of, made of?
Sugar and spice and all that's nice;
And that's what little girls are made of.

* * *

A smile beats a barrel of liver medicine.

A Resourceful Bird

"You wish to enter the diplomatic service. Can you give any proof of discretion?"

"Yes, I once entered a bathroom where a lady was in a bath."

"Yes, and what did you do?"

"I said: 'I beg your pardon, sir!' and withdrew."

* * *

Moonshine Liberality

You think that your luck was pretty good,
Then you find that it's rotten,
And you regret that you can't forget,
The swig you got for nottin.

* * *

Sunday School Teacher—"Now, children, who was sorry that the prodigal son had returned?"

Bobby—"The fatted calf."

* * *

O. F. Folks

(From the Albion, Pa., News)

H. J. Barns and E. F. Briston, accompanied by their own wives, were Cleveland visitors last Thursday and Friday.

* * *

You Win the Rubber Prize!

Lecturer (in a loud voice)—I venture to assert there isn't a man in this audience who has ever done anything to prevent the destruction of our vast forests.

Man in the audience (timidly)—I've shot woodpeckers.

* * *

We will now sing, "He Asked For Bread," and the curtain came down with a roll.

Passing of "Sappho"

IS THE theatre becoming immoral? The majority of critics claim it is. The Whiz Bang disagrees on this point. We claim the motion picture development has stopped the sporadic growth of suggestive plays on the legitimate stage.

The immoral, or at least suggestive, plays made their first appearance in any large number twenty years ago. Witness "Three Weeks," "Sappho," "Du Barry" and others, and still today you will find these plays in oblivion. Together with them, the women who starred in such plays are almost unheard of today. Most prominent among these is Olga Nethersole.

She was an English governess in the eighties and startled England with her portrayals of "The Transgressor," "Magda" and other productions of like character.

Twenty years ago Miss Nethersole shocked two continents with her "Sappho Kiss." She always maintained that playing the parts of these easy women would "make" her. Witness her interview to the Minneapolis Journal more than six years ago, in which she is quoted as having said:

"People have not understood that I chose to play prostitutes because I have felt it my work to aid the world by showing the suffering in it. If I felt that I had not been chosen for this task I should never have given my life to it.

"Do you know the story of Alexander Dumas, the younger? He was an illegitimate son, whose father refused to wed his mother. Thereupon the son gave up his life to the cause of woman and wrote his plays with the suffering of woman uppermost. 'Camille' will live forever.

"I have felt that if I should show the suffering and the misery that illicit passion causes I could do something for the world, could point a way toward removing the evil."

And today, Olga Nethersole's prediction has fallen flat. Her name, or the names of her mimics, no longer are blazoned on the electric signs of Broadway. Olga Nethersole, and the principle for which she stood, are in oblivion.

* * *

The Whiz Bang Sailor

Oh! I've washed my feet in the Ganges,
And me neck in the Bengal Bay,
    And I've tramped for miles
    In the Andaman Isles,
For less than a dollar a day.

Got lost in the Indian Ocean,
So typhooned it down to Bombay
    On the hurricane deck,
    Which I grabbed on spec,
In lieu of a few days' pay.

Was washed ashore at Haiti,
Got ironed out next day,
    So I quit the fleet
    Without wetting me feet,
And tangoed to Mandalay.

Got choked in old Calcutta
With the loss of a full day's pay
For taking a whack
At a policeman's back,
When looking the opposite way.

Sand-bagged in dusty Cavite,
Woke up on the low highway
And lived for a week
On the smell of a leek,
'Cause I had no monish to pay.

Fever and ague at Malta,
Sea sick right down to the knee,
Got chucked overboard
For allowing me Ford
To creep up the captain's sleeve.

Got spliced to a Chinkie in China,
And a Maltese in Malay,
And played ping-pong
With Miss Hong Kong
When me mothers-in-law were away.

Kidnapped in Ramal Pindi,
Exchanged for a bale of hay,
So I dilutes me beers,
With crocodiles' tears,
As I've nought all else to say.

* * *

Don't you recognize that lonely old woman weeping over there in the corner? She is the woman who, not many years ago, declared she would not be bothered with children.

* * *

Something to Worry About

A duke's coronet has eight strawberry leaves.

* * *

Ship Ahoy!

(Sign in millinery shop)

Wanted—Girls to trim rough sailors.

* * *

A Pullman porter has just compiled a book on Berth Control.

Frankie and Johnny Blues

Frankie and Johnnie were lovers,
Great Gawsh how they did love;
Swore to be true to each other
As the shining stars above.
He was her hubby,
But he done her wrong.

Frankie was a good woman,
Almost every one knows;
Saved up all of her money
To buy her daddy some clothes.
He was her patootie,
But he done her wrong.

Frankie lived in a nice home,
Kept her hair up in curls,
Gave her money to her loving man,
To spend on those boulevard girls.
He was her man,
But he done her wrong.

Frankie went down to the corner,
To buy herself some near-beer,
Says to the handsome bartender,
Has my loving man been here?
He is my man,
But he's doing me wrong.

I ain't going to tell you no story,
Ain't going to tell you no lie,
Johnnie left here an hour ago
With a party called Nellie Bly.
He is your husband,
But he's doing you wrong.

Frankie went back to the Bly house,
Didn't go back there for fun,
Underneath her red kimona,
She carried a 44 gun.
She's after the man
That was doing her wrong.

Frankie walked up and down State street,
Frankie was looking high,
In the window of a Chink shop,
She saw a man and Nellie Bly.
He was her man,
But he's doing her wrong.

Frankie knocked on the door,
Frankie pushed on the bell,
Open that door you "crooked girl,"
Or I'll blow you clear to—well,
You've got my man,
That's doing me wrong.

Frankie cracked Johnnie once,
Frankie cracked Johnnie twice,
The third time Frankie hit Johnnie,
He yelled, Oh, Cheese'n Mice,
You're killing your man,
That was doing you wrong.

Roll me over once, doctor,
Roll me over so slow,
Roll me onto my right side,
Those pellets hurt me so.
She finished her man,
That was doing her wrong.

Bring on your rubber-tired hearses,
Bring on your rubber-tired hack,
Take my daddy to the cemetery,
But bring his wrist watch back,
Best part of my man,
That done me wrong.

Thirteen girls dressed in mourning,
Thirteen men dressed in black,
They all went out to the cemetery,
But only twelve of the men came back.
They left her man,
That had done her wrong.

The last time I saw Frankie,
Frankie was looking fine,
Diamonds as big as horse eyes,
The owner of a big gold mine.
She was minus her man,
That had done her wrong.

* * *

Our Latest Song Success

Never Mind the Bread, Mother—Father Will Soon Be Home with a Bun.

Speed 'er Up

Johnnie, coming home from Sunday School, asked his mother if they had automobiles in heaven.

"Why?" asked his sweet mama.

"Because," replied Johnnie, "Just before leaving Sunday School everybody sang 'If We Love Him Here Below He'll Take Us Home On High.'"

* * *

Big Bill

Big Bill is a good old soul
As all of us will say,
No matter how the wind may blow,
His heart is always gay.

When Bill was young and in his prime,
A ladies' man was he;
Among the merry maidens sweet,
A long wide path cut he.

But now the silver in his hair,
Tells forty years and ten,
And chasing chickens, Willian finds,
Quite different now from then.

Alas, how sad the change it is,
And gone is all his vim,
For now when Bill goes out a night,
The next day he's all in.

And when he sits him down at noon,
To eat his simple meal,
'Ere he has tasted half his lunch,
Sweet slumbers o'er him steal.

And when some fellow jogs his arm,
He wakes with feeble smile,
Then lights his pipe and puffs and puffs,
And sleeps some more awhile.

At first his eyelids start to droop,
Then sags his lower lip,
And then out from between his teeth,
His pipe begins to slip.

Ah! good old Bill! 'tis sad to see,
The meaning all too true,
That when the pipe slips from his lip,
Big Bill is slipping too.

* * *

When the flesh is willing the spirit is seldom weak.

* * *

When he squeezes you tight in his loving embrace,
Till the thought of it makes you feel bold.
Do you shrink from his arms, kick him off the place?
It is not the custom I'm told.

* * *

Some men are so constructed that they just have to swindle somebody, and rather than be idle they will bunco their friends.

* * *

A Matter of Environment

I met a girl in Washington,
Employed in the mint;
I took her out to dinner
And she ordered without stint;

It cost me twenty dollars,
But I'll know enough next time
To get a girl who's working
At Woolworth's "Five and Dime."

* * *

Japanese Custom

A Japanese woman was brought into the police courts one day, carrying a little, chubby, red-haired baby in her arms.

During the course of the testimony the Judge asked her if the child's father was red-headed. She replied, "Me no savvy, honorable husban keep hat on."

* * *

"Fares, please," said the conductor as he slipped a few in his one way pocket.

Whiz Bang Editorials

"The Bull is Mightier Than the Bullet."

IN THE earlier days of our married life, Mrs. Bill was quite often embarrassed at the underground words of comfort offered her for her pain and suffering in bringing forth five bouncing babies into this world of sin and sorrow. Our neighbors were quite solicitious for her welfare and some even ventured so far as to infer that I must be more or less "brutal" or words to this effect. I'll admit that a set of twins the first year and three more young farm-hands in the ensuing four years was "going some."

At last, however, I have been vindicated and the vindication comes from no less a personage than the Honorable Arthur Brisbane, who insists that many children mean real happiness, and the greater the number the greater a mother's chance for living in history. He further says that "The real business of a woman, her highest business, whatever she may want or believe, is having children.

"This earth depends on the human race, and there can't be anything more important than the creation of that race.

"Women forget that sometimes, and not satisfied to create the man that does the work, they want to be the man.

"A woman may do as she pleases, nobody has the right to lecture or exhort. If she wants no children, that is her business.

"Few women voluntarily let the chain snap at their link. Two children replacing mother and father should be the minimum, and one day that will be the maximum, when the earth is fully populated.

"You learn from Galton's studies of heredity that among kings, and the very rich, the first child is apt to be the best. In humbler families the later children are the best. The reasons are plain.

"When a king marries, it is a novelty. He is interested in his first child.

"That child is born with all the king's affection and energy back of it. By the time the second arrives, he is tired of the mother and thinking of something else.

"Alexander the Great, first child of a great man and an extraordinary woman, was a huge success. Had there been a second, it might have been a half idiot, for by that time the mother hated the father and the father was afraid of the mother, who later had him murdered for taking a second wife.

"Among humble mortals the later children are the best. As time passes, and the husband grows older, he recovers from early foolishness.

"He appreciates the devotion of the mother

that has lived with him and stood by him, he becomes more nearly worthy of her, and so she gives him better children.

"You find this everywhere in history. Only earnest, intense affection produces the best children.

"Franz Schubert, the greatest of all song writers, was the fourteenth of fourteen children born to his mother.

"Guiomar Novaes, greatest of woman pianists, was the seventeenth of nineteen children born to her mother; and Caruso was the youngest of nineteen children.

"What happiness the world owes to the mothers that created those three great musicians! You can imagine how often those mothers were asked 'Why do you have so many children, why aren't you satisfied?'

"If Caruso's mother had stopped at eighteen children, or Schubert's mother at thirteen, the loss for the world would have been incalculable.

"Letis Ramolino had every excuse for wanting a small family. With her husband, Carlo, she traveled about Corsica amid wars and unrest. But if she had been content with a small family there never would have been any Napoleon Bonaparte. And the history of the last 125 years would have been different.

"If at first you don't succeed, try, try again. The oftener you try, the better chance you have of a really great success. That applies especially to motherhood."

* * *

Genuine drunkenness is the reel thing.

That Tool House On the Farm

By Budd L. McKillips

I have been in spacious buildings,
  Like the New York hippodrome,
But I've never seen the equal
  Of a place that stood near home.

I can see it near the garden,
  Very small but full of charm,
'Twas a place of boyhood pleasures,
  I remember on the farm.

Just a little wooden building,
  Where my daddy one bright day,
Found me seated proudly puffing
  On a rank, old pipe of clay.

It was there I kissed the hired girl,
  And she bit me on the arm;
It was there I pulled my loose tooth
  In that tool house on the farm.

* * *

Short and Snappy

A Rookie, doing his first night of guard duty, was suddenly approached by the officer of the day. The officer walked up to him and asked what his general orders were.

Rookie—Don't know.

Captain—What is the number of this post you are walking?

Rookie—Don't know, Captain.

Captain—Well, good night!

Rookie—Good night, Captain.

* * *

Love's Old Sweet Story

When a boy says "Will you?" and the girl says "Yes,"
The whole world changes in that one caress.
It's the same old story, the rest you can guess,
When a boy says "Will you?" and a girl says "Yes."

* * *

The eternal triangle—two dogs and a bone.

An Epilogue

Will you? Won't you? Can't I coax you?
Oh, come on, I think you might.
You know you said you would,
Or would not, be
My wife.

* * *

His Protecting Prayer

A celebrated revivalist came to address his flock, and before he began to speak, the pastor said: "Brother Jones, before you begins this discourse, there are some powerful bad negroes in this here congregation, and I want to pray for you," which he did in this fashion:

"O Lord, gives Brother Jones the eye of the eagle, that he may see sin from afar. Glue his ear to the gospel telephone, and connect him with the central skies. Illuminate his brow with a brightness that will make the fires of hell look like a tallow candle. Nail his hands to the gospel plough, and bow his head in some lonesome valley, where prayer is much wanted to be said, and anoint him all over with the kerosene oil of Thy salvation and set him afire."

* * *

So beautiful she seemed to me,
I wished that we might wed.
Her neck was just like ivory,
But, alas! so was her head.

* * *

"Ah was thinking," said Rastus Johnsing, "what a nice, peaceful laike world dis here universe would have been if it wasn't fer de movements of the human underjaw!"

We have told you of the song entitled "The Stockyard Rag." Now the words to the "Stockyard Rag" are not so catchy, but, Oh, my—the air, gee it's bully.

* * *

George Liebst's Dope

Do right and fear no man,
Don't write, and fear no woman.

* * *

Spanish-American War Relic

(Sung to tune: "Tramp, Tramp, Tramp, the Boys are Marching.)

In that land of dopey dreams, happy, peaceful Phillipines,
Where the bolo man is hiking night and day.
Where insurrectos steal and lie, where Americanos die,
There you hear the soldiers sing this evening lay:

CHORUS.

Damn, damn, damn the insurrectos, cross-eyed Kackiack ladrones;
Underneath the starry flag,
Civilize 'em with a Krag,
And return us to our own beloved homes.

Underneath the nipa thatch, where the skinny chickens scratch,
Only refuge after hiking all day long.
When I lay me down to sleep, slimy lizards o'er me creep;
Then you hear the soldiers sing this evening song:

Social customs there are few, all the ladies smoke and chew,
And the men do things the padres say are wrong.
But the padres cut no ice, for they live on fish and rice,
Then you hear the soldiers sing this evening song:

* * *

Did It Ever Happen to You?

Merchant—Have you had any experience in chinaware?

Applicant—Years of it, sir.

Merchant—What do you do when you break a valuable piece?

Applicant—Well—er—I usually put it together again and place it where some customer will knock it over.

Merchant—You'll do.

Now the killjoys want to eliminate tobacco from the tournament. Why not pass a general law making all happy persons criminals, and be done with it?

* * *

You can't choose your own name, but you can pick your own teeth.

* * *

When the donkey saw the zebra, he began to switch his tail,
"Good-night," he said, with frightful mien, "there's a horse that's been in jail."

* * *

A pretty girl in her first season is the nearest thing to perpetual motion yet discovered.

* * *

The case of two heads being better than one is exemplified in the barrel.

* * *

Another Dream

And when I was a damsel I dreamed as a damsel, and unto me the most dreaded of all words was the word "Spinster!"

But now that I am a wife I understand as a wife, and all my sufferings are the sufferings of a wife—and lo?

* * *

"This," said the goat, as he turned from the tomato can and began on the broken mirror; "this is indeed food for reflection."

* * *

Mrs. Milton: "And is her husband kind to her?"

Mrs. Stilton: "Oh, very! Why, he's more like a friend than a husband!"

* * *

A woman tells fairy stories to her children to quiet them. A man tells fairy tales to his wife for the same reason.

Prayer of the Doughboy

"Give us this day our long-delayed pay,
"And forgive the bugler, the mess sergeant, the Y. M. C. A.,
"And all those with bars on;
"And lead us not into the army again,
"But deliver us from all service stripes;
"For thine is the Army,
"The M. P.'s,
"The Q. M. C.'s,
"And the A. S. C.'s,
"Forever and ever. Amen."

* * *

Society Notes

The society columns of a Calgary paper claim the following interesting items:

Peter Jabberwock, of Didsbury, is in the city on a big drunk.

Miss Maude de Vere, of Drumheller, arrived in the city Wednesday and was run out of town the same night. It is a pity that Miss de Vere is not a racehorse, for she is very fast.

* * *

You may be deaf, young man, but you will get your hearing in the morning.

* * *

Wed men tell no tales.

* * *

We will now sing a song entitled, "Since Rebecca swallowed a spoon she cannot stir."

* * *

The mule hates the tow path. That is where he draws the line.

* * *

A bore is a person who talks so much about himself that you don't get a chance to talk about yourself.

Ten Nights In a Milk Store

The Things They Mix and Shake and Freeze Would Give a Man the Old D. T.'s—Delica Tessens.

By D. T. Fisher

Joe's coffee shop was crowded,
All the regulars were there.
About the door there stood a score
Who couldn't find a chair.
My Buddy Brown had just put down
His seventeenth root beer
And big McCann, the taxi man,
Was drinking cherry cheer.

When in there crept a dirty bum,
"Who'll buy a drink?" said he,
"For poor old Lou? Thanks friend, I knew
I'd find a sport. You see
In days gone by I traveled high.
My shirts were made of silk,
And all was well before I fell
For chocolate malted milk."

"It was drink that made me wretched, boys,
I went the pace that kills.
They robbed poor dad of all he had
To pay my soda bills.
My mother doped my coffee, yes,
And prayed for me at night.
But I'm afraid that lemonade
Was master of the fight."

"I'll never forget the night I met
That little blonde in blue.
She said, 'I'll take a nectar shake'
And I said 'Make it two.'
'Twas sweet and thick (without a kick)
And flavored strong of quince.
I'd never tried the stuff before
But how I've killed 'em since."

"I used to say that I could drink
Or let the stuff alone
Just as I chose. But heaven knows
I liked each ice cream cone
That I consume confirms my doom.
Its far too late to mend.
My clothes I'll soak for one more coke.
And speed the bitter end."

"And now you know my story, boys,
Plain soda suicide.
It's made me what I am today
I hope it's satisfied.
Just one request—when Satan's best
Have rushed me to the ropes,
Oh, be a friend in need and send
Me down my chocolate dopes."

* * *

Going Slow

The two men were adrift in an open boat and it looked bad for them. Finally one of them, frightened, began to pray.

"O Lord," he implored, "I've broken most of Thy commandments. I've been a hard drinker, but if my life is spared now I'll promise Thee never again—"

"Wait a minute, Jack," said his friend. "Don't go too far. I think I see a sail."

* * *

Any Replies? You Tell 'em!

(From Duluth Herald)

Desk Room and Stenographer for rent. Address A 239 Herald.

* * *

Girls now-a-days are very much like salads —a great deal depends on the dressing.

* * *

Our Old One Revamped

Since prohibition came, my wife made me likker.

* * *

Two things in this world you can't keep down—a good man and a bad oyster.

* * *

For Private Circulation

"May I print a kiss upon your lips?"

"Yes, provided you promise not to publish it."

Make It Snappy, Satan

"Get thee behind me, Satan,"
We cry with indignation.
"Get thee behind. Thou'rt much too slow,
For the modern generation."

* * *

According to
MRS. WIGGS

It ain't no use putting up your umbrella till it rains.

There ain't no use dying 'fore your time comes.

Looks like everything in the world comes right if we wait long enough.

* * *

Dad's stock of booze is getting low;
With care he removes the stopper,
And takes a little nip just so,
Out of a medicine dropper.

* * *

Just Say "Hullo"

"W'en you see a man in woe
Walk right up and say, 'hullo!'
Say 'hullo' and 'how d'ye do!'
'How's the world a usin' you?'
Slap the fellow on his back—
Bring your hand down with a whack;
Waltz right up, an' don't go slow,
Grin an' shake an' say 'hullo.'"

* * *

"Bobby," screeched his mother, "don't let me hear of you shooting crabs again. Those poor little things have just as much right to live as you."

Naughty, But Nice

I want the lights that brightly shine;
I want the men—I want the wine.

I want the fun without the price;
I want to be naughty and yet be nice.

I want the thrills of a long close kiss;
I want the things the good girls miss.

I want the arms and heart of a man—
And yet—stay single if I can.

Now can you give me some good advice;
How to be naughty and yet be nice.

* * *

Recently I received a request for information as to the size of my Whiz Bang farm, and in response to same, I wish to say I never have measured it. However, it covers so much ground that when I send a newly married couple out to milk the cows, they send the milk back with their children.

* * *

Ohell!!!

Eve corrupted Adam with it.

William Tell set a world's record with it.

The small boy risked a whipping for it.

The American people extracted the juice from it.

Congress took the joy out of it.

* * *

A friend in need generally needs too much.

* * *

As Uncle Even says:

"It's better to agree wif a man as much as you kin. It makes him feel good natured and you don't have to listen to so much talk."

Eh, Boys!

Tis sweet to love, but Oh! how bitter
To court a girl and then not gitter.

* * *

Who was that gentleman I saw you with today?

That wasn't a gentleman. He is my husband.

* * *

Les Nomes de Femmes

A chap I know calls his girl "Key-hole" because she something to adore (a door). Another friend calls his wife "Crystal"—not because he can see through her, but because she is always on the watch.

* * *

Let's now sing, with all the alcoholic accuracy possible, that old familiar farmer's wail: "I've got enough money to last me the rest of my life, providing I die tonight."

* * *

The only way some men can get ahead is by raising cabbage.

* * *

A boil on the stove is worth two on your back.

* * *

A friend of ours remarks that a lad with a full cellar has a lot of boozem friends.

* * *

Wow!

There was a young man named O'Dair,
Who would make a good diver, I swear,
For a minute like this
He'd hold a sweet miss,
And ne'er once would he come up for air.

* * *

The Sucker's squawk is music to the gambler's ears.

Those Styles

"That woman has a daub of paint on her nose."

"Well?"

"Shall we tell her about it?"

"Better not; it may be the latest style."

* * *

Hell is a heluva place for a heluva good fellow to have a heluva good time at a heluva price for a heluva long time.

* * *

Last year I asked "HER" to be my wife and she gave me a decidedly negative reply, so to get even I married her mother. Then my father married the girl .

When I married the girl's mother, the girl became my daughter and my father married my daughter, so he is my son. When my father married my daughter she became my mother. If my father is my son and my daughter is my mother, who am I?

My mother's mother is my wife and must be my grandmother and being my grandfather's husband, must be my own grandfather.

* * *

Our Pr. Blues

I want to be a doctor with prescriptions all my own,
To write them out and flop about,
As dead as any stone.
I'd love to be a physician and have my little nip;
Oh, I want to be a doctor—
And sip, and sip, and sip.

* * *

The front door of the business man's office says "Push." The front door of the city hall says "Pull."

One Thing He Hadn't Done

It was at a revival meeing. An old darky rose to his feet.

"Brudders an' sisters," said he earnestly, "You knows an' I knows that I ain't what I oughta been. Ise robbed hen roosts, an' stole eggs, an' to' lies, an' got drunk, an' slashed folks wi' ma razor, an' shot craps an' cussed an' swore, but I thank de Lord dere's one thing I ain't nebber done—I ain't nebber lost ma religion."

* * *

Lettuce See

Her pretty pink knees were unsocked,
As into the garden she walked.
The spuds, in surprise,
Shook the dirt from their eyes,
And even the sweet-corn was shocked.

* * *

One day Pat was riding a mule at the county fair grounds, when the mule, in jumping around, happened to get one of his hind feet caught in the stirrup. Pat saw it and said: "Say, you son-of-a-jack rabbit, if you're going to get on, then I'm going to get off."

* * *

Nosey Love

I went to see my girl one night,
For her love I was seeking,
I missed her mouth and kissed her nose,
The gosh darn thing was leaking.

* * *

A man often is judged by the company he keeps, but a woman must be judged by the time she keeps them.

Whiz Bang Monologue

My wife and I are very happy. In ten years of married life, we have had only one quarrel —and it's still going on. We were married at a little place called Pleasantville. It should have been called Battle Creek. Before we were married, I told her she had beautiful teeth. She hasn't closed her mouth since. I remember very well, the night we were married. She came up the aisle, supported by her father— yes, he supported her that night, but I've been supporting her whole family ever since. It was a hot, sticky night, and as we stood before the altar, the minister said to me, "Wilt thou?" I nodded. He said to her, "Wilt thou?" She nodded. Then he told us to clasp hands—and we both wilted.

* * *

"Hot Dog"

While fiery flames caressed his neck.
The dog stood on the burning deck,

* * *

"Have you anything to say before leaving the stand," asked the judge, after pronouncing a death sentence upon a negro murderer.

"Yes, suh, jedge," replied the prisoner. "I wants to say right here dat dis is gonna be a lesson to me."

* * *

"Young man, were you trying to catch that train you were just running after?"

"No, no; I was merely chasing it out of the station."

I Would, Wouldn't You?

Supposing that a man, avaricious and old,
Should come to me jingling his silver and gold,
And offer a share of his mansion to me,
If I to the sale of myself would agree,
I wouldn't—would you?
Supposing a hero, all bristling with fame,
And big with the weight of a wonderful name,
Proposed in a moment of blank condescension,
To give me his hand and a little of attention.—
I wouldn't—would you?
Supposing a youth, with his heart in his eyes,
That shone like the light of the beautiful skies,
Should promise to love me, through all his glad life,
And begged that I be his own little wife—
Guess I would—wouldn't you?

* * *

A great many very excellent jokes have their grounding on the mechanical error of a typesetter, but it remained for a proofreader on a Wichita paper to win the diamond studded stomach pump. Here is the manner in which Miss Higgins' silvery voice was described:

"Miss Higgins, after her graduation, will devote some time to the study and cultivation of vice. She has given her friends much pleasure along that line in the last two years."

Oh, Tempore! Oh, Hell!

* * *

Ike Marvel drew "Reveries" out of a cigar—Uncle Sam draws revenues, but if you want the biggest inspiration and income, you must hit the opium pipe. Opium puts you to sleep, but quickens your brain as De Quincy and Coleridge both prove. Opium dreams are in a unique class, aesthetic, supernatural and literary.

* * *

There is all the difference in the world between holding a wonderful hand and holding a hand wonderfully.

WE WERE gathered about the fireplace in one of the log cabins at Pequot the other night, seeing who could tell the biggest lie. A guest, whose first name was Mike won the rubber covered stomach pump. He told of the first bear he had ever killed.

"I was on a deer hunt near Pine River, about 10 miles north of here, with a doctor from Wheeling, W. Va.," was the way Mike started it.

"The doctor was more experienced in hunting deer, so he placed me on a 'run' where I'd get a thrill, while he scouted up the animals. I had been there about half an hour and was nearly on the verge of 'buck fever' when a big black bear crossed the 'run' in front of me. I managed to raise my rifle and to fire almost point blank at 'Bruin.' Then I stood as if glued in my footsteps. In a moment there was a hand placed gently on my shoulder and I heard my good friend the doctor say: 'Stand still as you can, Mike, while I go and get a spade.'"

* * *

Our Pets

When I got up in the morning,
And looked upon the wall,
The bed bugs and the roaches
Were having a game of ball.

The score was 20—0
The bed bugs were ahead,
The roaches started fighting,
And kicked me out of bed.

* * *

The next time you have a sore throat be glad you're not a giraffe.

Remember, Buddy

By Earle S. Keedy.

I danced with you in my arms,
They called you Rose,
You were indeed a wild rose
As you smiled o'er your absinthe frappe.
I listened as you told tales of gay Paris,
The Boulevards—Montmarte.
You smiled as you told your story
And lingered over the liquors;
The band played a wild fantastic air.
Oh, God! with you in my arms!

Then you talk of war—
Murder and blood and hate.
My! what a vicious little creature you are.
But ma cherie, we shall not talk of war tonight;
We shall dance and drink and smile and love,
Garcon, apportez encore de l'absinthe s'il vous plait.

* * *

You may pick beautiful strains on a mandolin for an hour and the girls don't even look out of the window, but just one honk of a horn—Oh, boy!

* * *

REALLY, Soaks, I don't know who to credit this little gem of poetry to, but it is so humanly interesting that I cannot resist the temptation to repeat it.

There was a man who loved the bees—he was their dearest friend. He used to sit upon their hives, but they stung him in the—end.

* * *

He Drinks Hair Tonic

He asked me if I'd kiss him,
I kissed him once or twice,
I know I hadn't ought to,
But, my Gawd, he smelled so nice.

* * *

Eczema, Oh! Eczema, don't be so rash.

Ode to King Nicotine

Tobacco is a filthy weed—
  I like it.
They say it fills no normal need,
  I like it.
It makes you old, it makes you lean,
It takes the hair right off your bean,
It's the worst damn stuff I've ever seen,
But—I like it.

* * *

A little bit may scorch the lips, but half a jag is better than none, according to the old toper.

* * *

A beer-keg, a cellar,
A jolly good feller,
Who always works with a will.
He used to loaf on any job—
But now he's got a still.

* * *

There's no use in trying to figure out women. A friend in New York writes that every time a woman gets one of these short skirts she also buys a hair net.

* * *

Our Autumn Girlies

With heads all bobbed like well kept hedges,
And knee-high skirts with scalloped edges;
In place of silken hose with clocks,
Their dimpled knees gleam o'er their socks;
The petticoat is out of style,
And corsets hardly worth the while;
They sit with limbs crossed, 'round the hall,
It makes our old time burlesque pall;
For there the girls, perforce wore tights,
But in these days, Oh Boy! what sights.

* * *

Every chicken likes corn. Some prefer it shelled from the cob, while others are willing to drink it right out of the bottle.

Throughout the day, a hen's a hen,
It's funny that I boost her.
For when night comes she mounts a roost
And then becomes a rooster.

* * *

Not Particular

(From Marion, Ind., Chronicle)

For rent—Sleeping room, for man and wife or young lady. Close in. 807 S. Boots.

* * *

A charming young belle of the Sioux
Stooped over to lace up her shioux,
But she said as she laced,
"I must have these replaced,
For I see they no longer will dioux."

* * *

You Name It, Boys!

Oh! girls, I have some news for you,
I'm married so beware,
To flirt with me would never do,
So darn it, don't you dare.

I know your little hearts will sink,
'Tis fate, Oh, fate is mean,
I'm handsome, but I really think,
I'm crazy in the bean.

* * *

She Missed It Too Late

From the Waco, Texas, News Tribune.

Lost—Between Sanger's and Goggan's on Austin street, a yellow organdie dress. Phone 1417.

* * *

She Asked Him

"Can you tell me, John," asked the fair young teacher, "where shingles were first used?"

"Yes'm," answered modest Johnny, "but I'd rather not, ma'am."

Separation

By Ella Wheeler Wilcox

HE

One decade and a half since first we came,
With hearts aflame,
Into Love's paradise, as man and mate;
And now we separate.
Soon, all too soon,
Waned the white splendor of our honeymoon.
We saw it fading; but we did not know
How bleak the path would be when once its glow was wholly gone;
And yet we two were forced to travel on—
Leagues, leagues apart while ever side by side,
Darker and darker grew the loveless weather,
Darker the way.
Until we could not stay
Longer together.
Now that all anger from our hearts has died
And love has flown far from its ruined nest,
To find sweet shelter in another breast,
Let us talk calmly of our past mistakes
And of our faults—if only for the sakes
Of those with whom our future will be cast,
You shall speak first—

SHE

A woman would speak last—
Tell me my first grave error as a wife.

HE

Inertia, my young veins were rife,
With manhood's ardent blood, and love was fire,
Within me. But you met my strong desire
With lips like frozen rose leaves—chaste, so chaste,
That all your splendid beauty seemed but waste,
Of love's materials. Then of that beauty
Which had so pleased my sight;
You seemed to take no care; you felt no duty
To keep yourself an object of delight,
For lover's eyes. And appetite
And indolence soon wrought
Their devastating changes. You were not,
The woman I had sworn to love and cherish.
If love is starved what can it do but perish?
Now will you speak of my first fatal sin
And all that followed, even as I have done?

SHE

I must begin,
With the young quarter of our honeymoon,

You are but one,
Of countless men who take the priceless boon,
Of woman's love and kill it at the start.
Not wantonly, but blindly. Woman's passion
Is such a subtle thing—woof of her heart,
Web of her spirit; and the body's part
Is to play ever but the lesser role,
To her white soul;
Seized in brutal fashion,
It fades like down on wings of butterflies,
Then dies,
So my love died.
Next, on base Mammon's cross you nailed my pride,
Making me ask for what was mine by right,
Until, in my own sight,
I seemed a helpless slave,
To whom the master gave,
A grudging dole. Oh, yes, at times gifts showered
Upon your chattel; but I was not dowered
By generous love. Hate never framed a curse
Or placed a cruel ban
That so crushed woman, as the law of man,
That makes her pensioner upon his purse,
That necessary stuff called gold is such,
A cold rude thing, it needs the nicest touch,
Of thought and speech when it approaches Love,
Or it will prove the certain death thereof.

HE

Your words cut deep; 'tis time we separate.

SHE

Well, each goes wiser to a newer mate.

* * *

Bye, Bye, George!

Why his girl in the old home time gave him the gate:

(Letter)

* * * and my office here is in the northwest corner on the twenty-first floor. The cold wind is something fierce. Am afraid it will be rather difficult to keep warm when the colder weather of winter comes. I am thinking that soon I will have to get an experienced stenographer * * *

Mohammedan Bull

BY CAPTAIN BILLY

WOULDN'T it be a great joke if the spirit of old man Mohammed, founder of the Mohammedan religion, had strolled along Fifith Avenue in the 1921 Easter parade? I'll bet the old-timer would be shocked at the beautiful display of feminine charm and harm. While a kid on a North Dakota farm, I remember reading some "bunk" about this "wine and swine" belief. And it was mostly bunk, but even at this late date, I recall some of the Mohammedan line of chatter in reference to the female of the species:

According to the law of Mohammed, no part of a woman's body should be exposed to public view, from the crown of her head to the soles of her feet. (Bare backs, front and center.) A woman violating this law would have fiery robes around her body in hell. They are also forbidden to look upon a man.

Once upon a time, Mohammed, so runs the tradition, was sitting in his drawing room with his wives (he had only fourteen), and along came Omar of Medina, a blind man, to have an interview with him. No sooner was he seen at a distance than Mohammed asked the ladies to retire to the inner apartment. They objected, of course, saying, "What harm is there if we stay, for he being blind would not see us?" "But you would see him," replied Mohammed, "and it is just as unlawful."

Mohammedans in all parts of the world are very particular, therefore, to adhere to the strict injunction. Women are not allowed to go out in the open air, except the poor laboring classes, whom necessity compels to break the custom.

A Mohammedan catechism on moral subjects, written by a Hindu gentleman of high literary reputation, reads about as follows:

Q. What is the chief gate to hell?
A. A woman.
Q. What bewitches like wine?
A. A woman.
Q. Who is the wisest of the wise?
A. He who has not been deceived by a woman.
Q. What are fetters to men?
A. Women.
Q. What is that which cannot be trusted?
A. A woman.
Q. What poison is that which appears like nectar?
A. A woman.

I guess the ancient Mohammedans weren't so crazy, after all. But the hardest knock to fair woman comes in the form of a Hindu proverb which reads: "Women are a great whirlpool of suspicion, a dwelling place of vices, full of deceits, a hindrance in the way to heaven, the gate to hell." They also believe in the "depravity of women and the sanctity of the cow."

In closing, here's hoping Mrs. Captain Bill does not believe in the sanctity of this "bull" before it reaches the printer. To play safe, however, I'll emphasize that it's the Mohammedan belief, not mine.

* * *

'Tis Tough, Yea

I met him at a neighbor's ball,
We walked beneath the moon,
He made such violent love to me,
I thought I'd surely swoon.

I thought now I have met my mate,
With him I'll spend my life,
But just as we were going home
He introduced his wife!

* * *

And Then Again

I met her at a neighbor's ball,
We walked beneath the moon,
She made such violent love to me,
'Till she passed in a swoon.

I thought now I have met my mate,
She surely is my loved one,
But just as we were going home,
She introduced her husband!

* * *

English as She Is Shopped With

The housekeeper walked into the shop and rapped smartly on the counter.

"I want a chicken," she said.

"Do you want a pullet?" asked the shopkeeper.

"No," replied the housekeeper, "I want to carry it."

Simple, Ain't It?

An Englishman at Victoria, B. C., recently introduced something entirely new in the fishing line. He calls it "beer bottle fishing" and it certainly seems to have become very popular out on the Canadian coast. The sports are all going in for it.

You fill the little boat with as many cases of beer as it will hold and set out to sea. After drinking a bottle you attach a line with baited hook to the cork, recork the empty bottle and drop it overboard. If blessed with a reasonable thirst you will soon have dozens of bottles bobbing about on the water.

When a bottle bobs frantically up and down, you've got a fish. By evening your boat is full of fish and you are full of beer.

And there you are!

* * *

Famous Sayings

Lemme?
Why Not?
Cantcha take a joke?
Goodnight!!!

* * *

A Fine Judge

First Autoist—"I thought you said if I were sociable with the judge I could get off?"

Second Autoist—"Were you?"

First Autoist—"Yes. I said 'Good morning, Judge, how are you today?' and he replied, 'Fine—twenty-five dollars'."

* * *

When a hen lays, she shells out.

A Matter of History

BY UNCLE DAN RETLAW

JOE RUSSELL, colored, appeared before the grand jury of Gonzales county, Texas, and testified that a white man by the name of Bennett had been dealing monte with the negroes in the Elm Slough community.

Monte dealing was a misdemeanor and was barred by the statute of limitations after two years from date of offense.

Bennett met Russell several hours before the trial and said, "Joe, I understand that you are a witness against me."

"Yes, sah, Mr. Bennett, dey just fo'ced me before the gran' jury and I had to tell it."

"That's all right, Joe, I dealt the game, but it was THREE years ago. It was in 1896. Now, don't you let Walter shake you from '96."

By the time the trial came up Joe was on the outside of at least six or eight drinks.

"Who was present, Joe, when Mr. Bennett dealt the game?" he was later asked on the witness stand.

"Laud God-a-mi'ty man! Dere was all ob Elm Slough and a whole lot of niggahs from Peach Creek."

"When did Mr. Bennett deal the game?"

"Er, er—it wuz '76."

"Joe, was it 1876 or 1776?"

"It was 1776."

"Joe, I suppose that you saw George Washington, Thomas Jefferson, Benjamin Franklin and Patrick Henry betting at Mr. Bennett's game."

"Er—Boss, I don't know dem niggahs. I spec dey belonged to dat Peach Creek bunch."

Thereupon the prosecuting attorney said, "With the permission of the court I dismiss this case. Mr. Bennett, you are undoubtedly the oldest gambler in the United States. I have established the fact that you dealt a game of monte back in the days of Washington."

* * *

"Johnny," queried the Sunday School superintendent, "what do you know of the birth of Moses?"

"Please, sir, Pharoah's daughter said she found Moses in the bullrushes—but they all say something like that."

* * *

Some Cake Eater, What?

By Bill Francis

It is something that is cute and neat,
A small necktie, and patent feet,
A part in his hair; his pants pressed so,
Crumbs in his pockets instead of dough,
A small black derby, a cute pair of spats,
Goes to a dance and thinks he's the cats,
Stands on the floor like a lily so pure,
Some silly girl comes along and says "sure,"
She thinks he is lovely and acts so refined,
They get on the car and she pays the dime,
Now, listen, girls, we might like their ties,
But remember, our mothers married regular guys.

That Thirty-Cent Feeling

A college graduate was looking for a position of some sort. Entering an office he asked to see the manager, and while waiting he said to the office boy:

"Do you suppose there is an opening here for a college graduate?"

"Dere will be," was the reply, "if de boss don't raise me salary to t'ree dollars a week by tomorrow night."

* * *

'Tis tae Bade

An elderly Scotchman was up before the magistrate for being drunk and disorderly. He tried to explain that he had fallen into bad company.

"Tell us about it," said the magistrate, sarcastically:

"Weel," said the Scot, "I had two boattles o' whuskey and a' the ither men in the room were teatotallers."

"Discharged."

* * *

Boy, Page Mr. Wolstead

Ten thousand jooze,
Are making booze,
With government permission,
To fill the needs
Of a million Swedes
Who voted prohibition.

* * *

If a girl wants to do a little missionary work, she might go into the kitchen and help mother.

The Twin

There are two of us. My brother and I look so much alike that our own mother couldn't tell us apart. When we were at school my brother would throw spit balls, and the teacher would whip me. Of course, she didn't know any better, but I did.

My brother got into a fight, and the judge fined me five hundred dollars. Of course, he didn't know any better, but I did.

I was supposed to be married last Sunday, but my brother arrived first and married my girl. Of course, she didn't know any different, but I did.

However, I got even with my brother. I died last Monday and they buried him.

* * *

Our Monthly Motto

Have you a little Hell in your home today? (With apologies to the soapy fairy.)

* * *

A Lemon

An echo of the Stillman case is heard from Calgary, Alberta, in the following report:

A somewhat spicy Calgary divorce case is on the tapis. Mr. John A. Torgerson, resident across the Elbow, is the name of the gentleman who is about to sue for a divorce, the co-respondent being one Peter J. Lemon, a rancher. What makes the case a peculiarly sad one is the fact that a prattling babe was born into the family about a month ago. Friends have tried to effect a reconciliation for the sake of the child, but Torgerson remains adamant, insisting that his wife has handed him a Lemon.

* * *

To leave your umbrella in the vestibule of a church is a sure test of Christian faith.

The Little Red God

Here's a little red song to the god of guts,
Who dwells in palaces, brothels, huts;
The little Red God with the craw of grit;
The god who never learned how to quit;
He is neither a fool with a frozen smile,
Or a sad old toad in a cask of bile;
He can dance with a shoe-nail in his heel
And never a sign of his pain reveal;
He can hold a mob with an empty gun
And turn a tragedy into fun;
Kill a man in a flash, a breath,
Or snatch a friend from the claws of death;
Swallow the pill of assured defeat
And plan attack in his slow retreat;
Spin the wheel till the numbers dance,
And bite his thumb at the god of Chance;
Drink straight water with whisky-soaks,
Or call for liquor with temperance folks;
Tearless stand at the graven stone,
Yet weep in the silence of night, alone;
Worship a sweet, white virgin's glove,
Or teach a courtesan how to love;
Dare the dullness of fireside bliss,,
Or stake his soul for a wanton's kiss;
Blind his soul to a woman's eyes
When she says she loves and he knows she lies;
Shovel dung in the city mart
To earn a crust for his chosen art;
Build where the builders all have failed,
And sail the seas that no man has sailed;
Run a tunnel or dam a stream,
Or damn the men who financed the dream;
Tell a pal what his work is worth,
Though he lost his last best friend on earth;
Lend the critical monkey-elf,
A razor—hoping he'll kill himself;
Wear the garments he likes to wear,
Never dreaming that people stare;
Go to church if his conscience wills,
Or find his own—in the far, blue hills.
He is kind and gentle, or harsh and gruff;
He is tender as love—or he's rawhide tough;
A rough-necked rider in spurs and chaps,
Or well-groomed son of the town—perhaps;
And this is the little Red God I sing,
Who cares not a wallop for anything
That walks or gallops, that crawls or struts,
No matter how clothed—if it hasn't guts.

English Wit

BY PAUL VERE

I met a young lady friend the other evening, and it would be as well to remark here that she is no longer a friend of mine.

All innocence, she glibly asked: "Do you know Francis?"

"I couldn't claim the pleasure of his acquaintance, so gallantly I replied: "No, Francis who?"

"France is a beautiful country," she smiled.

Fool that I was to have fallen so easily into the trap, but I schemed for my revenge. A little later I calmly remarked: "Do you know Sonia?" She unsuspectingly answered: "No, Sonia who?"

" 'T's on'y a rumor!" I chuckled.

But how could I, mere man, hope to have the last word. A moment later the blow fell. "Do you know Hiawatha?"

"No," I groaned. "Hiawatha what?"

"I watha a good little girl till I met you," she purred.

I writhed inwardly, and for a moment was speechless, but even a worm will turn, and feebly I muttered: "Do you know Roland?"

She was very good about it. "Roland who?" she asked bravely.

"Roll and butter," I mumbled. Then before she could recover herself:

"Do you know Annie?" I cried.

She "bought" it like a hero—I mean heroine.

"Annie who?" she queried.

"Anybody," I gurgled.

Tauntingly she cooed: "Do you know Arthur?"

"Arthur who?" my teeth chattered.

"Our thermometer," she echoed.

In desperation I fired a final shot.

"Do you know Hugo?" I demanded.

"Hugo?"

"Hugo to —" But just then I remembered that I was a gentleman. I turned and fled.

* * *

The Tired Hired Man

Well, well, well, at last Gus, the hired man, has turned to poetry. With the able assistance of Maggie, the cook, he submitted the following orgy:

By Gus, the Hired Man

The hired man chases the bull o'er the field
His weary task to complete,
And the pale moon shines her mantle o'er
The golden shocks of wheat.
"I'm dry," he cried, with a snoose-parched throat,
As he blasphemed Heaven above.
"I'm far away from dear old Chi
And the bitter beer I love."
At the boss's call he turned once more
His row of shocks to scan
And said, "I am, 'tis just my luck,
A tired hired man."

His short night o'er, the moon hath raised,
Her waning light to show
The hired man a setting forth
On his day of toil and woe.
Full fourteen hours with scarce a rest,
He toils with heart so brave,
'Till reeling to his straw tick bed
He sleeps—a worn out slave.
Old pals who do in shy Chi dwell,
Think sometimes, if you can,
Of the weary, dreary, beerless days,
Of the tired, hired man.

* * *

A word to the wise is as good as a flea in the ear.

Who Lost?

Mr. Isaacstein approached a taxi driver and asked what would be the fare for himself, his wife and children to a certain address.

The cabby asked $2.50. Mr. Isaacstein offered to toss the cabby double or quits.

The cabby consented and won the toss, whereupon the would-be passenger turned to his wife and said, in despairing tones: "Just my luck, Rachel; now ve shall have to valk home!"

* * *

Our Sob Song

"This is my last 'shot'," murmured the bartender as he bumped himself off.

* * *

"Will your daughter make her debut at a ball?"

"No, something new. We're going to give a prize fight for the dear girl."

* * *

Which Are You?

Two men by the wayside sat,
And both bemoaned their lot;
The one because he had buried his wife,
The other because he had not.

* * *

I Carry Red Ink In My Pen

He—"I found this hairpin in my pocket. Is it yours?"

She (Severely)—"No, I use brown hairpins. This is black."

He (Brightly)—"Hm. Guess my fountain pen's been leaking again."

For Women Only

"'What knocked out that movie comedian?"

"Hit by a pie."

"Why, he is bombarded by pies every day."

"His bride threw this. It was one she made herself."

* * *

Kick Up Your Heels a Bit

If your back is sore and weary
From long sitting in a chair;
If your joints are getting rusty
And rheumatics make you swear;
If the ills of age assail you,
Or you're getting far too stout;
If your knees are getting wobbly
Or you're troubled with the gout;
If you're head is getting shiny
On the place your hair should grow;
If the little things annoy you
And make you suffer so;
It's time you took a tonic—
Get out, yell, and make a noise;
Take a day off from your labors
And spend it with the boys.

* * *

I Kissed You

Judging from the following poem from the pen of Victor J. Jones, we assume that Mr. Jones really kissed some rare and dainty fluffy flapper, but of course the reader may have doubts. It may be that Mr. Jones was only dreaming.

By Victor J. Jones

I moved a step closer, we stood face to face,
Shoulder to shoulder, my arms 'round your waist;
Her lips were a-quiver, so anxious and true,
To press close to mine, in a manner that you
Can only explain. I drank from her eyes
That heavenly bliss that men always prize.
A flower, a rose will wither and die,
But a scent like a kiss will never lie;
My lips still hold that charm as then,
And the first time we meet I'll smack you again.

The Passing of the Old Smokehouse

Well, Readers, here we are—in again. It seems next to impossible to keep this masterpiece of American literature from finding its way to the printed page. And so we republish James Whitcomb Riley's simple gem of rural life. You who have often scented the fragrant smell of the old fashioned farm smokehouse will surely appreciate this poem.—The Editor.

By James Whitcomb Riley

When memory keeps me company and moves to smiles or tears,
A weather beaten object looms through the mist of years.
Behind the house or barn it stood, a half a mile or more,
And hurrying feet a path had made straight to its swinging door.
Its architecture was a type of simple, classic art,
But in the tragedy of life it played a leading part;
And oft the tired traveler drove slow and heaved a sigh,
To see the modest hired girl slip out with glances shy.

We had our posey garden that the women loved so well;
I loved it, too, but better still, I loved the stronger smell
That filled the evening breezes so full of homely cheer,
And told the night-o'er-taken tramp that human life was near.
On lazy August afternoons it made a little bower,
Delightful, where my grandsire sat and whiled away an hour;
For there the summer mornings its very cares entwined,
And berry bushes reddened in the steaming soil behind.

All day the spiders spun their webs to catch the buzzing flies
That flitted to and from the house, where Ma was baking pies;
And once a swarm of hornets bold had built a palace there,
And stung my unsuspecting Aunt—I must not tell you where;
Then father took a flaming pole—that was a happy day—
He nearly burned the building up, but the hornets left to stay.
When summer bloom began to fade and winter to carouse,
We banked the little building with a heap of hemlock boughs.

But when the crust was on the snow and the sullen skies were gray,
In sooth the building was no place where one would care to stay;
We smoked our bacon promptly—there one purpose swayed the mind,
We tarried not nor lingered long on what we left behind.
That dear old country landmark; I've tramped around a bit,
And in the lap of luxury my lot has been to sit;
But ere I die I'll eat the fruit of trees I robbed of yore,
Then seek the shanty where my name is carved upon the door.

Our Censorship Program

With motion picture censorship in operation several of our "first runs" will look like a streak of rain after the official amputation by the censors has been made.

IF A HUGE fish is being caught and it makes the water shimmy—

"Deleted by the censor—no shimmying allowed."

If a bright youth is smoking a cigarette while making a record high-dive—

"Deleted by the censor as a bad example for boys and girls."

If the picture is supposed to have 10,000 school kids in it and the censors can count only 9,998—

"Deleted by the censors as not truthful."

If flames destroy everything but the bare walls of a building—

"It can't be shown—nothing bare shall be screened."

If in a train wreck the engineer breaks his leg—

"It can't be shown—nothing suggestive allowed."

And last, but not least, if the West Point cadets spell "Bears" in a novelty drill formation—

"Deleted by the censors—it suggests war."

Last But Not Least

Willie was a very bashful boy and always clung to his mother's apron strings. He would not run out and play with other boys and therefore was quite ignorant of the outside world. So Willie grew up this way and was now a young man, and still clinging to his mother.

There was a widow next door who had become friendly with Willie's mother, and one day she stopped to have a chat and they became engaged in a conversation which drifted into the bashfulness and homeliness of Willie.

The young widow then remarked that Willie ought to go out with the boys once in a while and then, too, he should visit with the girls a little bit. She then offered to take Willie and his mother to the picture show, but Willie's mother had some work to do and could not go. The young widow then offered to accompany him.

Willie blushed and said he didn't want to go unless mama went along but the young widow assured Willie's mother that she would bring him home safely.

Willie kissed his mother good-bye and told her he would be home early and so the mother said she would wait up for him. And she waited, and eleven o'clock came and Willie was not home yet. She knew that the shows were closed by that time and she became worried. Twelve o'clock came and Willie was not home yet. About this time his mother fell asleep in the chair and was awakened by approaching footsteps at one o'clock in the morning. She knew that it was her Willie and she hastened to the door to greet him.

But Willie came in with his head bowed low and passed his mother without saying a word and went straight to his bed and began to cry. This was the first time that Willie had failed to kiss mother on returning home and she began to wonder what was wrong. She went to the bed where he lay sobbing and in tender words asked him what had happened.

Willie still cried and after the mother had managed to console him, she again asked what had happened. Willie said, "Oh, mama, Oh, mama, that young widow, that young widow," and he said these words as if his heart would break, "That young widow said that there ain't no Santa Claus."

* * *

Mary Ann Blues

The sun don't shine as it used to did,
The moon a mushroom seems;
The Naiads all have gone to sleep,
Beside the sluggish streams.
I sometimes counterfeit a laugh,
To make folks think I'm gay—
I've got the scruter-nutics bad,,
For Mary Ann's away.

Peaches don't taste like peaches now,
I don't know pork from veal;
Moonshine, or mush and milk for me,
Would answer for a meal.
There's Sally though—she'll cheer me up—
I'll visit her today,
And make arrangements for the time,
That Mary Ann's away!

* * *

"Please help the blind," moaned the beggar as he brushed a speck of dust off his coat sleeve.

Quack, Quack

"I sent a dollar to that fellow who advertised to tell how to take out wrinkles in the face."

"And did he tell you?"

"He did. He said to walk out in the open air at least once a day, and the wrinkles would go out with me."

* * *

The Naked Teddy

The fierce-looking woman from Belgium stepped into a New York toy shop and gazed frigidly at the clerk who hurried to her side.

"I vants," she said, with a strong accent, "ze naked Teddy."

The poor clerk blushed hotly and thought wildly of his wife.

"Er—um, would you mind saying that again?" he stammered.

"Ze naked Teddy," persisted the lady. "You have him in ze window."

"Great Scott," gasped the clerk. "We'll have the police here in a minute. Come outside, madam, and show me."

Once outside, she pointed excitedly to a Teddy bear. "Zere you have him, what you call him, ze Teddy bare," she cried.

* * *

Country vs. City

"Hey, you! Don't stop your car near my horse! It skeers him."

"Don't worry, I know the rules. 'Don't park near a plug'."

Highty-Tighty Aphrodite

AT PRESENT, partly owing to what is very modestly called "barefoot" dancing, a severe season of clotheslessness prevails; and the aforementioned exercises afford the public quite a fair idea of "the most admirable spectacle in nature"—that is to say, bowlegs, knock-knees, thick ankles, spray feet, shoulders scraggy or pudgy, knees bony or lumpy, and wierdly shaped legs. So says the Picayune of New Orleans.

The modernist poets also have been seized by the mania for nudity—but let us hope that with them it is rather theory than practice; for the average literator is not usually "a dream of form in days of thought.". One mocking rhymester thus makes game of such poetic aspirations:

All the poets have been stripping,
Quaintly into moonbeams slipping,
Running out like wild Bacchantes,
Minus lingerie and panties.
Never knew of such a frantic
Belvederean, corybantic,
Highty-tighty Aphrodite,
Stepping out without a nightie.

One of these modernist bards puts her own fancies into the brain of an old-time lady, stiff in pink and silver brocade, as she walks in a prim garden awaiting the coming of her suitor. She would like to leave "all that pink and silver crumpled on the ground"; for

Underneath my stiffened gown
Is the softness of a woman bathing in a marble basin.

Thus divested of raiment, "I would be the pink and silver as I ran along the paths," and her lover, seeing her, would pursue "till he caught me in the shade." A writer of free verse is more candid; it is herself she would disrobe. "Since the earliest days I have dressed myself in fanciful clothes," she says, trying to express herself in this manner; but now she is weary of putting "romance and fantasy into my raiment," she realizes that "my clothes are not me, myself"; hence the stern resolve:

I think I shall go naked into the streets,
And wander unclothed into people's parlors.
The incredulous eyes of the bewildered world,
Might give me back my true image, * * *
Maybe in the glances of others,
I would find out what I really am.

Doubtless she would; but perhaps not exactly as she means it. Wandering "unclothed into people's parlors," if police vigilance could be eluded, might be a way of seeing ourselves as others see us, since the owners of the parlors would probably be startled into candid comment, instead of, as usual, waiting until the unclad back of the visitant was turned. It would be a happy arrangement if only the truly symmetrical would indulge in semi-nudity. Such exhibitions are a form of female vanity; but if the average woman will but realize it, she owes any admiration she may excite to the saving graces of clothes. If she is wise she will foster the illusion. As a poet of another era expressed it, "Oh, the little less, and what worlds away!"

* * *

Can a Dead Cat Smell?

OUR neighbor's twelve-year-old daughter was walking down the country lane the other day, carrying an armful of goldenrod. Gus spied her and at once was curious.

"What are you doing with the goldenrod?" he asked.

The little girl replied that she was taking it to her cat's funeral.

"Why, that's foolishness, Gertie, to take flowers to a cat's funeral," insisted Gus. "A dead cat, you know, doesn't smell."

The little girlie shook her tousled head in disgust as she answered back: "Why, Gus, you've got no imagination at all."

And Gus doesn't know yet what she meant.

* * *

Safety First

Her Daughter—"Mama, you know that phonograph record that you had made of your voice?"

Mrs. Henpeck—"Yes."

Her Daughter—"Well, whenever you're away, pa puts it on the machine and sasses it something awful."

* * *

"How very unusual," mused the garage keeper, as he swept the street while cursing the drayman.

WELL, well, well, will the agitation over the whiffenpoof ever end? Here's the latest, from John Easalier: "A whiffenpoof is an attachment a cross-eyed man wears so that when he cries the tears will not run down his back."

* * *

There are three joys on this earth,
That we men can't forget,
They appear to be a woman's kiss,
A drink or a cigarette.
Each one seems to call for more,
To each one there is "class"
But, brother, if I had my pick—
Just put mine in a glass.

* * *

In a Rose Garden

A hundred years from now, dear heart,
We shall not care at all.
It will not matter then a whit,
The honey or the gall.
The Summer days that we have known
Will all forgotten be and flown;
The garden will be overgrown
Where now the roses fall.

A hundred years from now, dear heart,
We shall not mind the pain;
The throbbing crimson tide of life
Will not have left a stain.
The song we sing together, dear,
The dream we dream together here,
Will mean no more than means a tear
Amid a Summer rain.

* * *

"I call this dress a crime," said Hupp.
Replied his storm and strife:
"Stop jawing now and hook me up."
So he fastened the crime on his wife.

* * *

"I'll be dammed," said the brook, as the tree fell across it.

Oh, Dear, Such Is Life

"What's the matter with your wife?" She's all broken up lately."

"She's got a terrible jar."

"What has happened?"

"Why, she was assisting in a rummage sale, she took off her new hat, and somebody sold it for thirty-five cents."

* * *

A Minnesota man has a dog that chews tobacco and still has some sense left. But it doesn't drink hootch peddled these days.

* * *

The old saying "Here's How" used to refer to drinking the festive spirit. Now it applies to making it.

* * *

Laugh at every man's joke; tell none of your own; believe all fish stories; don't snore; pay cash; and you'll be fairly popular.

* * *

Sad But Too True!

"I was once prosperous, ma'am," said the tattered visitor.

"What did you do for a living?"

"I owned a cure for inebriates."

"And I suppose prohibition put you out of business?"

"Yes, ma'am. People who have been drinking hair tonic, benzine and varnish need the services of a regular doctor."

* * *

Taking an Interest

(From the Cincinnati Inquirer)

WANTED—Middle-aged man to take half interest with lady in rooming house.

OUR friend, Stew Lewis, says that our dope about the "clean joke" in the August issue should have read as follows:

"May I hold your Palm, Olive?"

"Not on your Life, Buoy, we've a 'Little Fairy' in our home already."

* * *

The Sailor's Beloved

From "Our Navy"

A gay and handsome sailor man,
Lay on a bed of pain,
All hope had passed; his life ebbed fast,
Ne'er would he rise again.
"Have you no sweetheart fair and true?"
They whispered o'er his bed,
"Whom you would tell a last adieu?"
The young man softly said:

"There's Betty back in Bremerton,
Juanita in Mexico,
There's Sally in Seattle town
And Beatrix in Bordeaux;
At Hampton Roads there's Harriet,
Whom I must surely see;
And Nellie, too, at Newport News,
Please bring them all to me."

The watchers stared in wild surprise,
And then they said once more:
"Come, tell us pray, without delay,
The girl that you adore;
The girl whom you have sworn to love,
And bring both wealth and fame;
Your promised wife—your hope and life,
Quick, let us hear her name."

"There's Lily at Long Beach," he said,
"And Daisy, dear, in 'Diego',
There's Lucy in Los Angeles,
And Pauline in San Pedro,
Barbara, dear, in Brooklyn
And Susie in St. Paul."
The young man sighed, "It's time I died;
I've sworn to wed them all."

Our History Lesson

George Washington and Abraham Lincoln both were born on holidays.

* * *

A Woman's Answer

A fool there was, and she lowered her pride,
(Even as you and I)
To a bunch of conceit in a masculine hide—
We saw the faults that could not be denied,
But the fool saw only his manly side
(Even as you and I)
Oh, the love she laid on her own heart's grave
With the care of her head and hand
Belongs to the man who did not know
(And now she knows that he never could know)
And did not understand.
A fool there was, and her best she gave
(Even as you and I)
Of noble thoughts, of gay and grave,
(And all were accepted as due to the knave)
But the fool would never her folly save
(Even as you and I)

* * *

Brethern and sistern, our text fo' today will be taken from the book of Whiz Bang, chapta fo' 'leven fo'ty fo', verse seben 'leben: "He who sitteth on a red hot stove shall rise again."

* * *

No man can knock a show harder than the guy who goes in on a pass.

* * *

A kiss is not a feast; it is an invitation to the feast.—J. Randolph.

* * *

Whether it's cold or whether it's hot,
We must have weather whether or not.

* * *

And now a gob from the U. S. S. Mississippi opines that farmers and hunters are not the only ones who use "shot guns." How do you get that way, Jackie?

IT CERTAINLY is surprising, the progress present day children are making towards manhood and womanhood. A few days ago I met Neighbor Wilson's boy, Freddie, on his way home carrying a package.

"You'd better hurry, Freddie, or you'll be late for dinner," I said, and to my surprise the kid blurted out:

"Tuhel I will, I've got the meat!"

* * *

A pretty young girl named Lenore
Was buying some hose in a store:
"How long " asked the clerk,
With a sort of a smirk,
And she answered, "From here to the floor."

* * *

Another Famous Saying

When in Rum do as the Rummies do.

* * *

"What a dead place," remarked the tourist as he surveyed the cemetery.

* * *

MAGGIE, the hired girl, says she overheard Mabel North tell her best friend yesterday that she sure "hooked 'em fast last week," and we have been wondering if Mabel referred to a fishing trip or her usual Saturday night stroll down Main Street.

* * *

The difference between a country youth and a city youth is that the former wants to know everything and the latter thinks he knows it all.

* * *

Many hands make light work—also a good jackpot.

In Quest of A Wife

OUT of the shadows of the far past comes this bewitchingly simple story. Like all the narratives of the Bible, it eclipses the most magnificent imaginings of the world's greatest novelists.

The story is that of a father commissioning his servant to go in quest of a wife for the heir of the house, and of the servant's rich find among the relatives of his master, and of the return to Abraham's tent in Canaan with the prospective bride, and of the fair maiden's warm and loving reception by Isaac, and of Isaac's joy and comfort in having a wife to share with him his wealth.

If other men had been in Isaac's place, it is probable that they would have wished to make their own choice of a life companion. But Abraham knew what he was doing that day. So he directed his servant to secure a suitable wife for Isaac.

Meanwhile, let there be suggested some practical lessons for the present age. We need help in our companionships. Abraham's servant went forth in search of Isaac's wife with his lips flowering in prayer. That man recognized the fact that marriage is a serious business. It was right that he should ask for assistance.

Too many marriages in these days hinge on a pair of brilliant eyes, or the curve of a pair of scarlet lips, or the gracefulness of a form; the young man being captivated by mere physical beauty, fancying that he is getting a thornless rosebush, but often finding that he has planted a deadly nightshade in the garden of his life. So has many a young woman been charmed by a handsome face, or broad shoulders, or courtly manners.

We need to be careful that marriage be more than an affair of boyish caprice and girlish romance. When marriage is born of lust, or when it becomes naught but a bargain, there can be no happiness beneath the roof-tree under which it has joined its mismated souls.

We need help in the conduct of business. This was a matter of business that here concerned Abraham's steward. Not only must he choose a maiden whom Isaac would be likely to love at first sight, but he must choose one who would not lead Isaac astray. The beautiful Rebekah was the answer to his prayer, who made Isaac an excellent wife, though in her old age we see some things in her character not above criticism. But where can perfection be found among mortal clay?

* * *

Had Everything Else

"Cherie," said the sergeant on pass, "how'd you like to take my name?"

"Non," said Fifi, thoughtfully, "I sink I ought to leave you somesing."

Girlie Girls

There is something that is getting to be awfully scarce in this world. Shall I tell you what it is? It is girls. That is what is missing out of the sentimental, breathing, living world just now. We have lots of young ladies and lots of society misses, but the sweet, old-fashioned girls of ever so long ago are vanished with the poke-bonnets and cinnamon cookies.

We want home girls—girls who are mother's right hand; girls who can cuddle the little ones next best to mamma and smooth out the tangles in the domestic skein when things get twisted; girls whom father takes comfort in for something better than beauty, and the big brothers are proud of for something that outranks the ability to dance or shine in society.

Next, we want girls of sense—girls who have a standard of their own regardless of conventionalities, and are independent enough to live upon it; girls who will wear what is pretty and becoming and snap their fingers at the dictates of fashion when fashion is horrid and silly; girls who will not smoke and drink, or accept hospitality from chance acquaintances.

And we want good girls—girls who are sweet, right, straight out from the heart to the lips; innocent and pure and simple girls, with less knowledge of sin and duplicity and evil doing at twenty than the pert little school girl at ten has all too often; girls who say their prayers and love God and keep his commandments.

She, Too?

William J. Burns, the noted detective, said in a Scranton lecture:

"To a well-trained detective every incident is pregnant with significance—yes, every incident is as full of meaning as—well, I am reminded of a story:

"A young man sat in a parlor alone. To him a beautiful girl entered. Thereupon the young man arose, took six cigars from his upper waistcoat pocket, laid them carefully on the piano, and then advanced toward the girl passionately, his arms outstretched."

But the girl drew back.

"You have loved before," she said.

* * *

In this issue a girl, who withholds her name, gives a little sonnet. We believe it one of the snappiest of its kind, considering its brevity, yet given to the anxious public. The thoughts of the writer are easily read between the lines. She writes:

My parents told me not to smoke;
I don't.
Nor listen to a naughty joke;
I don't.
They told me it was wrong to wink
At handsome men, or even think
About intoxicating drink;
I don't.
To dance or flirt was very wrong
I don't.
Wild girls chase men and wine and song;
I don't.
I kiss no men, not even one—
In fact, I don't know how it's done;
You wouldn't think I have much fun—
I don't.

* * *

When a wife fights her husband's will, he isn't necessarily dead.

The Jazz Dance

BY JOSEPH SCHNEIDER

YES, MA'AM, Terpsichore old girl, I've snared the latest dope on this here dance question and I'm going to hand you and our readers the newest line of palaver, that was ever chattered by an authority on high-stepping, meaning, of course, myself. As you know, every first-class essay, what this is going to be, has to have what has been nicknamed an exposition of the proposition, which translated in common sense means a correct explanation of the thing you are trying to explain. So to make myself clear, I'm going to hand you one of "them" expositions, which is guaranteed to kill at one hundred paces with all funeral expenses paid. With this clarifying admonition, a nickname for advice, prepare for a Christian burial.

As you ought to know, but probably don't, a phenomenon is one of those things in nature, that is, because it has happened and happens because it transpires. There is no reason for phenomenons except that they got to be. Well, we had one of them phenomenons at the village hall the other evening and I was there. Fellows, what haven't got a poetic license calls it a dance, but what's the use being unoriginal.

In the olden days, they used to call it a ball, for the reason that he grabbed she and then they rolled around a little. But that hasn't got enough pep, punch or originality anymore and besides it's no fun rolling around, seeing it's after July 1st. So what those tall-stepping "waltz hounds" up and does, but calls it a jazz festival and gets away with it.

Well, when they start to inaugurate this combination grizzly-b u n n y-hug-shimmee-she-wabbling festivication, me and Kid Herpercide was standing in front of the glide emporium just about the time the jazz artists .were ready to shake the raggy rhythm out of their bazoo-kaphones. Says the Kid, "Les git in on a little of this joyful novelty noise." Says I, "All right," doing the "wife" act, fumbling through my pocket, leaving on as how I left my pocketbook t' home. The Kid didn't fall for it, so I knows it's up to me to "ooze" in on my face, knowing that I was taking advantage of the zoo-keeper, being as how I am so handsome. The Kid plants down a berry and a dime, what is explained as a bonus to Uncle Sam, because he let us help him win the war. There was a guy at the door, that slipped all those jazz demons what produced the kale, a blue ribbon countersign which gave everyone of them "cuckoos" the priviliginous right to love up his neighbor's wife and hug each "sweet thing" with impunity which is another way of saying, that he can use both arms, without haffen to pay the judge for it in the morning. Well, I slipped by this animal keeper at the front gate, as I was completely disguised behind the ambuscade (the camouflage term for long whiskers) of a three weeks' shave and he thinks maybe I was a bulshevik or a anti-saloon leaguer or something like that. And I wants to state with firm insistantation right here, even if I has sank so low as to drink red pop and vote the democratic ticket, no one can slip me the accusation that I ever associated on intimate terms with the barbers.

Well, I wasn't in that jazz parlor more than half a minute, new time, when I lamped the bird, that must be at least second cousin to the gink what discovered the "shimmy." I figured in a flash that he was the sensation of the evening. The more I looked at that "fufu" writhing in blissful agony, the more I felt sure that he was the sensation of a coupla seasons. Now, I know he's the sensation of the last three centuries. Old man Noah had this bird of paradise on the job when he led the baby kangaroo down the gang plank of the ark, else how could a kangaroo walk that way.

I grabbed me an education watching this jazz sensation and the female creation that played opposite him get under way. He slaps a high and fast one around her neck. She chucks an inshoot to his ribs. He follows up with a wicked one about the belt. The sliphorn manipulator draws a bass obligato groan out of his slippery slide, the drummer beats the life out of a cow bell and the piano man just whips them ivories to death And like a big boat getting started, he and she shivered their way through the varying states of hesitation to the final degrees of perfect "shimmy-ing." There are rules that govern every jazz movement and direct every wabbling maneuver; you do not move the feet. Wonderful snake-like movement, controlling every muscle from the shoulder to the knee. You wiggle your left fin like the St. Vitus dance and pose your right shoulder like the rock of Gibraltar. He puts his sweaty face on she and she puts her powdered cheek on he. It's easy. No work at all. Don't even have to stand up. She braces you and you brace her like two rifles at stack arms.

I gave this stuff the eager eye while the ladies and their male escorts perspired and sweated and expended energy and the orchestra tunefully kidded old Man Music into believing that he was like old wine, getting better with age. And when the harmonics ceased to continue, a lantern-jawed swain, with nothing on his mind but his pompadour, juffawed "more, more," like he was asking for seconds in the chow-line at the corner saloon.

On with the dance. I looks up and there is Kid Herpercide himself stepping 'er off and telling lies to a peroxide individual of feminine characteristics who wore a red neck-tie. The Kid was plumb loco and I accumulated so much disgust that I sneaks to the Watch Dog of the Treasury, what guards the shekels at the door and demand my money back. And not getting it, I goes out under God's canopy (class to that poetry, eh, Terpsi) and tells my troubles to the stars.

* * *

Chicken Fever

By Field Ashworth

Broke, broke, broke,
    But it sure was some night, O Gee,
My tongue is thick and fuzzy,
    From the stuff they sold to me.
It's jake for my lady guest,
    I think she went south with my jack,
It was fine for the taxi bird
    Who motored us there and back.
Pink elephantines, I know,
    Didn't vanish July the first,
The devils danced on my bed all night,
    And I woke with an awful thirst.
Broke, broke, broke,
    I'm through with this rounding, right—
Damn that phone. "Oh, hello there, kid.
    Say, what're y' doin' tonight?"

* * *

Here's an old timer, rejuvenated for the occasion:

Rebecca was a fat woman and she and her husband, Abe, started to drive to town. A highway robber held them up, but Rebecca had managed to hide her rings and so saved them. After the robber had left, taking Abe's horse and buggy with him, Abe said:

"Rebecca, vere did you hide the rings?"

"In my stocking," said Rebecca, proudly.

"Mine Gott, for vy didn't you say so before. We could have saved the horse and buggy."

* * *

Electricity in Franklin's time was a wonder. Now we make light of it.

"Lasca"

I want fresh air, I want free life,
And I long for the cataracts and the cattle,
The crack of the whip, like shots in the battle;
The medley of horns and hoofs and heads
That wars and wrangles, scatters and spreads;
The green beneath, the blue above,
The dash, the danger, life and love—and Lasca.

Lasca used to ride on a mouse-grey mustang close to my side
With blue serape and bright belled spur,
Why! I laughed with joy as I looked at her;
Little she knew of books or creeds,
An Ave Maria sufliced her needs;
Little she cared, save to be by my side,
To ride with me and ever to ride,
From San Sabas shore to Lavatoes tide
In Texas, down by the Rio Grande.

Her eyes were of brown, a dark, dark brown,
Her hair was darker than her eye,
With curled crimson lip and instep high;
You could tell there ran in each vein,
Mixed with this milder Aztec strain,
The vigorous vintage of old Spain.
She was alive in every limb,
With feeling to her finger tips;
And when the sun is like a fire
And the sky one burning blue sapphire,
One does not drink in little sips
In Texas, down by the Rio Grande.

She was as bold as the billows that beat,
She was wild as the breezes that blow,
From her little head, to her little feet,
She was swayed in a supplelet to and fro
By each gust of passion, like a trembling pine
That grows on the edge of a tangent bluff,
And wars with the winds when the weather is rough,
Is this Lasca, this love of mine?
She would hunger that I might eat,
Take the bitter, leave me the sweet.

But once when I made her jealous for fun
In something I whispered, said or done,
With another girl I used to know
That belonged to the tribe of the Alamo.
She drew from her garter a dear little dagger
Alike the sting of a wasp it made me stagger.
An inch to the left, or an inch to the right,

And I shouldn't be maundering here tonight.
But she sobbed and sobbingly so swiftly bound
Her torn ramoso about the wound,
That I quite forgave her—well, scratches don't count
In Texas, down by the Rio Grande.

The air was heavy, the night was hot,
I sat by her side and forgot, forgot,
Forgot the herd that were taking their rest,
Forgot that the air was close, oppressed,
That the Texas northerns come sudden and soon,
In the dead of night, or the blaze of noon,
And once let that herd at its rest take fright
There's not a thing on earth can stop its flight.
And woe to the rider and woe to the steed
That falls in front of that mad stampede.

What! was that thunder?—No.
I sprang to the saddle, she clung behind.
Then away on a mad race down the wind
And never was horse pressed half so hard
And never was steed so little spared,
For we rode for our lives,
And you shall hear how we fared
In Texas, down by the Rio Grande.

The mustang flew, but we urged him on,
There's one chance left and you have but one—Halt!
Jump to earth, shoot your horse, crouch under him,
And hopelessly take your chance;
And if those steers in their frantic course
Don't batter you both to pieces at once
You may thank your stars, if not, alas, good-bye
To the quickening kiss, the long drawn sigh,
To the open air and the open sky
Of Texas, down by the Rio Grande.

The cattle were gaining and just as I felt
For my good six-shooter behind my belt,
Down came the mustang, and down came we, clinging together.
What was the rest? A body that spread itself on my breast,
Two arms that shielded my dizzy head,
Two lips that hard on my lips were pressed.
Then came thunder into my ears
And over us hurled that sea of steers,
And blows that beat blood into my eyes,
And when I could rise—Lasca was dead.

I gouged out a grave a few feet deep
    And there in earth's arms I laid her to sleep,
Where she is lying no one knows,
    The summer comes and the winter goes.
For many a day the flowers have spread
    A pall of petals over her head,
And the little grey hawk hangs aloft in the air,
    And the sly coyote trots here and there,
And the rattle snake glides and glitters and slides
    Into a rift in the cottonwood tree,
And the buzzard soars on, comes and is gone,
    Stately and still like a ship at sea.
And now I wonder why I do not care
    For the things that are like the things that were,
Does half my heart lie buried there?
    In Texas, down by the Rio Grande.

* * *

The Tale of a Tail

If the ghost of Oliver Goldsmith could only gaze today upon the economical skirts of the modern woman he would smile at the Goldsmithian ranting of a few generations back when he declared that nothing could be better calculated to increase the price of silk than the present manner of women's dress. "A woman's train is not bought but at some expense," says this eminent writer, "and after it has swept the public walks for a few evenings, is fit to be worn no longer; more silk must be bought in order to repair the breach, and some ladies of peculiar economy are thus found to patch up their tails eight or ten times in a season."

Ye Gawds. Imagine the modern female filibuster patching up her tail eight or ten times (or even once) because of the undue length of her outer lower garment. No chawnce, Chauncey.

Direct From Denver

Had we not heard so much of the Denver coughing college yell it would be difficult to believe that the girls of the Colorado summer resort ever ask permission to kiss a fond farewell smack to their loved fiances. According to the latest story to ruminate through the hacking, healthful mountain air, a pretty but shy young woman approached the information desk of the Denver Tourist bureau at the Union station recently. Mrs. Pearl Hobbs, the clerk in charge of the information desk, looked up to inquire in what way the bureau could serve her.

The girl separated from her escort and drew Mrs. Hobbs to one side.

"That young man," confided the girl, "is my fiance. We are to be married in a few days. He is going away on the next train and I wanted to ask you if it would be proper if he were to kiss me good-bye in front of all those people out there."

Mrs. Hobbs was nonplussed. While the questions she answers cover a wide range, this was a poser.

"Why, I suppose it's all right," said Mrs. Hobbs. "It all depends on the way you look at it."

Apparently the young girl and her fiance looked at it in the right way, for just as the train was about to pull out there was a quick, sharp smack—and the crowd wasn't so badly shocked.

Monkey Mongrels

ONCE again there is hope for us wicked, wilful and weak-minded men who have reaped and garnered the harvest of a misspent life. Hope dangles on the theory of the implantation of a monkey gland. Hell's bells, Doc, hand us two or three glands at once. But be sure you get us the 1922 model of monkey.

As we absorb the story about this monkey gland, it is touted as a magic that will put the jazz in seventy-year-old feet, restore white or grizzled locks to their pristine hue, iron the wrinkles out of the cheeks, off the forehead and away from the eyes, fill up the cavities in the neck, straighten the bent spinal column, steady the hand that wields the pen, put ginger where chalk is in the joints, make the pulse beat firmer and faster, paint a sunrise flush on the face—in short, give a man all the "vim, vigor and vinegar" that an athlete can use in his business.

One skeptical newspaper paragrapher says he won't take any stock in the gland story unless somebody can show him that it will make an octogenarian climb a tree and leap nimbly from bough to bough, clinging the while with strong hands to whatever holds him up. That, perhaps, is asking too much, seeing that the tastes of very few men, young, middle-aged or old, run to tree-climbing. It should be proof enough of the virtue of the monkey gland accessory if, when attached, warmed up and set to work, it makes a human mechanism of the vintage of about 1840 want to break the speed record and hustle past all the old danger signals that Nature had reared along the course.

Just as some of us were bucking up hope of youth renewed like the eagle's, Dr. William Mayo is quoted as saying in New York that he never heard either of the Paris scientist, or of the particular gland referred to. It is possible, of course, that the 1922 model of monkey, unlike his anthropoidean quadrumanous mammal ancestors, has this attachment and that a specimen thus equipped has not fallen under the observation of American scientists, although we have been reading about glands warranted to upset the venerable itinerary of Mother Nature.

Anyway, like a drowning man, we'll grasp at the last straw because we vainly desire to follow that motto: "Our step is pep; our creed is speed." Place your gland orders early, all you old timers, and remember that the older the buck the younger must be your monkey glands.

* * *

Life is like the old-time wooden pump—you have to prime it if you expect to get results.

That Shiftless Shavetail

He was a very young "shavetail" who looked as if he should be wearing knee breeches.

One day, when his company was up for inspection at the training camp, one of the men remarked in a tone of deep sarcasm, "And a little child shall lead them."

"The man who said that, step forward," was the immediate command. The entire company stepped ahead.

The lieutenant looked up and down the line. "Dismissed," he announced shortly.

The men thought that they had got the better of him, but not for long, for that night at retreat when the orders for the following day were read, they heard: "There will be a twenty-five-mile hike tomorrow with full equipment, and a little child shall lead them on a damned good horse."

* * *

Ain't It, Though!

Pat to Mike—"Did you hear that England was going to set Ireland free?"

Mike—"They are?"

Pat—"Yes."

Mike—"And we don't have to fight for it?"

Pat—"No."

Mike—"Ain't that just like the dirty English?"

* * *

The caterpillar is content with his lowly lot because something tells him he will soon wear wings.

Peril in Kissing

Attorney General Gregory tells this story on a financier and a physician:

The Money Juggler called at the office of the physician and told him with much concern that his only son was suffering from sore throat. The doctor was solicitious, but assured the financier that with the care given in the hospital to which the boy had been sent he would pull through nicely.

"But," said the father, "the boy confessed to me that he is sure he caught it from the parlor maid, whom he had kissed."

"Well, young people are certainly very thoughtless," mused the doctor. "I'm sorry to hear that your son has been so indiscreet."

"Yes, of course, doctor," said the financier, nervously, "but, don't you see, to be frank with you, I've kissed the girl myself. Do you think I, too, will have the disease?"

"Why, yes," said the doctor. "You are probably already infected. In fact, that would be the very next thing to expect."

"Oh, that's awful," gasped the financier. "I kiss my own dear wife every night and morning, and she, too—"

"Good heavens," cried the doctor, "then I'll have it, too."

* * *

Don't worry because men roast you; it may be they need the exercise.

Patience is the greatest of all shock absorbers in this mortal life.

Our Own Fairy Queen

A group of the fellows were raising the deuce,
In the tea room of Chester McVeigh,
And Horace Van Alstyne was acting a goose
While sipping a caramel frappe.
Back of the counter in an apron of white
Sat stunning Percy La Due,
And watching his movements with eyes filled with love
Was Luther McVicar Depew.

Then into the place a tripping there came
A fellow as handsome as sin,
And without even nodding or giving his name
He asked for a box of sen-sen.
That the boys were amazed you can readily see
For no one knew what he would do,
But we were all pacified, when he ordered us tea,
Except Luther McVicar Depew.

The stranger's eyes wandered over the place
Till the zither he spied on the chair,
Then a smile of contentment came over his face
And a blush hid his features so fair.
He strummed at the strings, with his fingers so white
(Though they could be a little more clean)
And then as we waited our eyes all alight,
He played "The Dance of Our Own Fairy Queen."

That he'd taken lessons there wasn't a doubt
For he played with an ease born of skill,
Till you almost imagined you were tripping about
On the banks of some rippling rill.
The tone of his music then suddenly changed
And he played for us "Little Boy Blue,"
I turned and there staring, his hair disarranged
Sat stunning Percy La Due.

The music then became very low
You scarcely could tell what he played;
It made the cold chills come over you, so
That you felt as you do when they raid
You could almost imagine a wrong had been done
And it made you feel nervous and blue,
While large pearly tears began to fall from the eyes
Of Luther McVicar Depew.

Then the dear boy arose and smiled at us all
As we applauded his efforts with vim,
Then for Percy McVicar he started to call
And he pointed his finger at him,

"Now, boys dear," said he, "You're not acquainted with me,
I might be a stranger that's true,
But one of you here is certainly fresh,
And that hussy is Percy La Due."

I nearly swooned at the words he had said
For I knew there would sure be a spat,
For when Percy is aroused he is nasty as Ned
And he scratches and claws like a cat.
I was certainly frightened, my nerves were a wreck,
I hardly knew what I would do,
For Percy was scratched on the face and the neck
And the musician had blood on him too.

Then Chester McVeigh pulled a police whistle out
And blew it real loud once or twice
The boys they all flew in disorder and rout,
I assure you it was not very nice.
Well, the police they came in and took Percy away,
The musician he went along too;
But the one who was punished severely that day
Was Luther McVicar Depew.

* * *

Intelligent Bugs

The farmers gathered outside the village inn were launching bitter complaints against the ravages of the potato bug.

"The pests finished up my crop in less than two weeks," said one farmer.

"They ate mine in two days," said another; "and then roosted on the trees to see if I'd plant some more."

A man who was traveling for a seed firm cleared his throat, and then interrupted, saying:

"That's remarkable, I own, but let me tell you what I saw in a town store. I saw a couple of these bugs examining the books, about a week before planting, to see who had bought seed."

Richest Man Found

I wonder if you knew that one of the richest men in the world lives in Pierce, Neb. That man is the writer. I am just a common plug blacksmith, but, oh, how rich. I go to my labors each morning, work until noon, go to dinner, return at 1:00 P. M. and work until 6:00 o'clock. I enjoy the greatest of all blessings—good health. Rockefeller would give all he possesses in money or holdings for my stomach, but he can't have it.

I have a most wonderful little wife. She has stuck to me twenty-two years now, so I know she must be a dandy to accomplish that. I have a little home, a beautiful little daughter, a son grown to maturity and now in life's game for himself. Rich? Why, man alive, who can possibly be richer?

Then, to add to all the above riches, I take down my old shotgun in season and ramble through the fields, woods and tangle in search of the elusive cottontail, teal and mallard, with my faithful old pointer at heel (now past eleven years old), and he is as happy as I when we are on the hunt. Then, when I get back, oh, how good everything does taste. Then when night has spread its mantle over this good old universe I settle down in a good, old easy chair, enjoy a smoke and then roll into bed to be embraced by Morpheus, and never hear a sound until the beautiful break of another day. Rich, did you say? Well, I guess. Dollars? No, not many. You inquired about riches, not material wealth.

The Fable of A Bug

THERE once was a Married Couple who gave birth to a Son, and when the neighbors discovered that the Child had Gold Teeth and a face like Willie J. Bryan, the Fire Whistles blew and the Bells on the First Baptist Church rang like mad as the Joyous Tidings spread from lip to lip throughout the Town of ----------.

The Great Jack ------ was born on the Rock-Bound Coast of ------, barefooted and with no clothes. Like most Boys of -------- He lived close to the soil and Day in, Day out, cultivated the paternal Potato Patch. In due time came the Great War. "Bullsheveeky," cried the Great Jack. So spoke the spirit of '98, but the Boy was married so He did not have to enlist in the Marines and So be the First to Fight, etc.

Little girls from His Wife's Sunday School Class strewed flowers in his pathway and when the Three O'clock Local pulled out everybody waved panamas as Jack went off to War. He wrapped his prehistoric Enfield around his neck like a pitchfork. He clashed his heels together like a Threshing Machine and Ripped out a Hand Salute that made the Captain shake and shiver as if Shell Shocked. He bawled out

Commands like a Twin Six exhaust and Hawkeye was his Middle Name.

And while it was written that other Non-Coms should spend their lives Drilling Blackboys in the Depot Brigade, not so with Jack. He was to be a Major General and Advisor and Right Hand Man to General Pershing.

MORAL—You Can't Keep a Good Rough Diamond Down.

* * *

The One Restraint

There was a meeting of the Powers That Be.

"I can't make a woman keep a secret," said Faith, despondently. "She promises to, and she really means to, but—it slips out somehow."

"Of course you can't. I can't do it myself," observed Discretion. "Goodness knows, if she won't do it for me, she won't for anybody."

"That's true enough," said Pride; "she won't even do it for me."

"Nor me," declared Shame.

"Nor me," sighed Honor.

"Nor me," wept Loyalty.

"Nor even me," asserted Policy, in a surprised tone.

"I can't make her do it," admitted Fear.

"I can't either," owned up Bribery.

"I can make any woman keep a secret," piped up a still small voice. And he who spoke was Illicit Love.—Town Topics.

* * *

A woman never dresses so carefully as when she goes to meet her best enemy.

Literary Indigestion

There is more truth than fiction in some of the stories appearing in American magazines. Arthur Somers Roche in the Cosmopolitan perhaps unconsciously reveals a time-worn trick of the woman of the streets in "working" a male victim. He writes:

The difficulty with the Waiters' Union had resulted in the engaging of girls as waitresses at the Central. An extremely pretty girl had just served Mr. Dabney with something. Inspiration had come to him as he started to tip her.

"Worth just fifty cents, m'dear, if I put it in your hand. Worth five dollars if I put it in your stocking. What say?"

The waitress essayed coyness, but failed in her endeavor. Five dollars is five dollars. She turned slightly to one side; her skirt was raised; into her stocking-top Dabney slipped the five dollar bill.

No invention of modern history has ever been acclaimed with the enthusiasm that greeted Mr. Dabney's strikingly original idea. There was a yell from Mr. Ladd's table; as explanation shot about the room, hilarity reached its highest pitch. Immediately a dozen girls stood close to tables, while unsteady hands that held bills fumbled at tops of stockings.

Baird's eyes were frightened as he turned to Miss Elsing. But he reconsidered his offer to take her home as he saw the mirth in her eyes, the broad smile on her lips.

The disgust left his own eyes. Honi soit qui mal y pense. After all, evil was in the thought not in the deed. It really, when you stopped to think of it, was something of a lark, this idea of Dabney's.

He reached into his waistcoat pocket as the waitress passed by him. He touched her on the arm. She turned, and her face was vaguely familiar. Somewhere, sometime, he'd seen her. But he could not place her now. He drew her near to him; he tipped her exactly as Dabney had done. The girl laughed, thanked him, and moved on. He turned to Eileen for approval.

"You warm up as the evening progresses," she told him.

Jimmy Ladd was settling with a head waiter for the party. Baird joined him.

"Hadn't we better have more wine?" he asked.

Obsequiously the waiter took his order. Five minutes later, the check was presented. Hotels are rather careful about these matters on New Year's eve.

* * *

Most Assuredly

The skipper had the rookie on the carpet. The rookie was hardboiled.

The skipper decided to take a fatherly attitude.

"If you were in my place," he asked, kindly, "what would you do?"

And right away came the answer: "Resign."

Water, Water, Everywhere

By J. P. McEvoy

Water is a wondrous blessing,
Good for washing necks and ears,
Just the thing for lakes and rivers,
Indispensable for piers.
Nice to park beneath the bridges,
Swell for making rain and ink,
Water is a wondrous blessing,
But it makes a ——— drink.

Water is composed of two gases, both dry, but which become wet when they get together. This often happens among men in dry territories.

Water is found in many places, such as oceans, lakes, milk stocks, on the knees, on the brain and recently on the bar. One becomes accustomed to having water in oceans, lakes and stocks, but water on the knee is something else again. However, this condition is easily cured by wearing pumps. If you suspect you have water on the brain, have a small hole bored into your head. If water runs out, you have water on the brain. If nothing comes out, you have no brains.

Noah was the first prohibitionist. He lived on water for forty days. The strain was too much for him, however, for as soon as he got out of the Ark, he beat it for the grape juice fermented, and drank himself cock-eyed.

Jonah was another of those ardent water spaniels. His story about the whale, however, casts some suspicion on him, and leads one to muse upon the kick the stuff must have had in those days.

Water falls upon us in the shape of rain, snow, hail, and water taxes. It springs out of the ground at the slightest provocation, and many places have both hot and cold running water and never have to pay a janitor for neglecting the furnace.

A large percentage of the human body is water. This percentage is rapidly increasing since the first of July. In the not far distant future burial will consist of being poured back into the ground.

* * *

And Watch It Fade

"The French," said Dr. Sidney E. Mezes, of New York, the brilliant director of the American peace delegation's experts, "the French are terrible cynics about love. They don't believe in its durability. They claim it never lasts.

"Two French poilus were discussing love in an estaminet.

" 'I hold,' said the first poilu, 'that if you fall in love with some ravishing beauty, the only way to cure yourself is to run off.'

"The second poilu took a sip of wine.

" 'Yes, that'll cure you, all right,' he agreed, 'provided you run off with the ravishing beauty'."

Pasture Pot Pourri

Feeling the Wheeling Ceiling

By Earl Girard

There was a young lady from Wheeling,
Who had a most terrible feeling,
The nurse rubbed her back
With a rough gunny sack,
And tossed her clear up to the ceiling.

* * *

In all of love's adventures, look before you kiss, for nothing is so easy as to marry in haste and divorce with pleasure.

* * *

Sign on a Barber Shop Window

DURING ALTERATIONS ON THE FRONT, CUSTOMERS WILL BE SHAVED IN THE REAR.

* * *

If you want to make light of trouble, keep it dark.

* * *

Last night I held a little hand
So dainty and so neat,
I thought my heart would surely burst,
So wildly did it beat;

No other hand into my soul
Could greater gladness bring,
Than that I held so tight last night,
Four aces and a king.

* * *

"Where are the glasses, the bitters, the mixer, the corkscrew?"

Oh, You Blues

Ashes to ashes and sand to sand,
If you want a lovin' daddy
Get a soldier man.

* * *

Sayings of the Famous

"Come on Seben."—C. Rastus Johnsing.
"Come Heah, Honey."—Mandy Smith.
"Up Jumped the Devil."—Abe Crapshooter.
"Hit Me."—Blackjack Pete.
"Gimme Two."—Poker John.
"Hands Up."—Profiteering Pete.

* * *

The man who knows all about women should forget it if he values his own peace of mind.

* * *

The mayor of Champaign, Ill., wires to the mayor of Rye, N. Y., that it is now a long time between, etc., etc.

* * *

It isn't necessary to call a man a liar. If he is, he knows it; and if he isn't, he isn't a man.

* * *

He was to take her for a trip in his new yacht the next day, and she was questioning him about it.

"How awfully nice of you to name the boat after me!" she giggled. "What is she like?"

"Well—er," he answered—"she's not much to look at, don't ye know, but she's very fast."

* * *

A girl in a taxi feels perfectly safe as long as the driver doesn't look around.

* * *

The lover who speaks but says nothing never faces a breach of promise suit.

Fable of A Maid

THIS being the complaint of a Maid who considereth a Husband. "Behold," counseleth my Mother, "thou hast become a Woman and must put away Childish things—

Therefore, take a Husband."

Would that I were destined to be a Spinster,

For then would I still believe that there existed, somewhere in this world, a man who was "Different."

Verily, from the first Smile to the last Kiss

They are as Hotel Soup—

From the same Stock, whatever its name or appearance.

Yea, whether he be as retiring as a Bridegroom or as bold as an insurance agent—they all falleth for the same line of chatter (with variations).

One Pursueth if I pretend to flee;

One pretendeth to flee if he thinketh that I Pursue;

And if I run not after him, cometh back to see what is the matter.

I raise my Voice in supplication and ask,

How now shall I choose?

Shall it be the callow Youth, the Exponent of Terpsichore and Connoisseur of Woman,

And spend the remainder of my Days in Ironing his one silk Shirt and perfuming his bath?

Or shall I establish a Covenant with Real Man in the crude form

And spend the better part of my life in giving him a Polish,

And when I have turned out the "Finished" product to mine own liking

(And have grown tired and weary in the process),

Have him turn to the Philandering Flapper, Pure and Chaste (the less pure the more chased), for Compatibility?

Six things there are in Man which I abhor and the seventh my soul Detesteth—

Egotism, Poverty, Indifference, Tobacco Chewing, Ignorance, Snoring,

And Cynicism;

For tho' he speak with the tongues of Men and Angels, and hath not a sense of Humor,

How then shall he appreciate me?

There abideth, Faith, Hope and Charity these three;

I have Faith, there is Hope, and I imploreth Charity;

But the greatest of all is a Sense of Humor which overlooketh all—

And tho' I search for Nebo's lonely mountains, through the Land of Moab, to the Shores of the Seven Impassable Seas,

How shall I know Love when I have found it?

Verily, verily, I say unto you that I shall search until I have found a man with a true Sense of Humor;

Then, and not until then, will I fear "Kismet."

Selah.

BROWNIE

* * *

Uncle Silas Says:

The alimentary canal of the business world needs a physic. It's the same in business as with the human system, when things get clogged. We've been gorging the system of the business world until its tripe needs scraping. We've kept the hopper too full for a healthy elimination, and we need calomel and rhubarb for a change. Capital has allowed its cormorant-like propensities to assume the proportions of a boa-constrictor in trying to swallow not only the calf but the whole herd. Labor, following closely in the wake of capital and profiting by its example, has pulled the bridle off of the horse and started it down the road of reason for a head-on collision with the captain of industry, who is stepping on the tail of his big Packard, and both will be injured.

Cornering the earth and setting the price of all things required for man's welfare has come home to roost in demands for wages double and treble what they used to be, and both capital and labor must be purged of this overload on the liver of righteousness or the undertaker will have an unusually thriving business very soon.

Plump Polly Puckers

Plump Polly, possessing pathetic past, participates proudly, preparing pancakes, pastry, persimmons, pie, pickerel, pea puree.

Parsimonious Paul perspires perpetrating passe piano pieces, perforce poverty, providing plenty profanities per pious prudish persons.

Portly Polly prefers perfect phonographic peace.

Paul's position prompts proud posing. Purpose promote pleasant prattle per peevish Polly.

Purpose Prostrated.

Paul performs perilous penury, pawning priceless platinum pendant, procuring proceeds preparatory purchasing perfume pleasing Polly.

Pseudo Paul pawns, purchases, presents.

Pert Polly permits pulse palpitation.

Psyche's promotion powerfully progressive.

Polly pines possessing Paul's pulchritudinal physique.

Prodigious Paul proposes perpetual partnership.

Pair pet, press, pucker.

Proof—Perseverance pays.

—Edgar M. Schonenberg.

* * *

Hail, Hail

Hail, Hail,
The Gang's all here.
Mustn't say that naughty word.
Mustn't say that naughty word.
Hail, Hail,
The Gang's all here.
Musn't say that naughty word,

Invoking A Hoary Fable

SOME six hundred years before the beginning of the Christian era, or perhaps long before that, a little fable was set afloat from Greece or Egypt or Arabia or Persia. It is most commonly called today "The Belly and the Members." Aesop—if there was such a man—may have sent it forth. At any rate, he or a chap of the same name is held responsible for this and scores of other fables.

There is something in this fable about "The Belly and the Members" that gives it piquancy and pertinence in these days of industrial unrest, of class consciousness and of a widespread feeling that the other fellow is getting all the best of it and that something drastic ought to be done to him to get out of his system his supposed Let-George-do-it notions; something to compel him to do his part of the chores of life. One popular up-to-date version of the fable—there are others—runs like this:

"One fine day it occurred to the Members of the Body that they were doing all the work and the Belly was having all the food. So they held a meeting and after a long discussion decided to strike work until the Belly consented to take its proper share of the work. So, for a day or two, the hands refused to take the food, the

Mouth refused to receive it, and the Teeth had no work to do. But after a bit the Members began to find that they themselves were not doing well. The Hands could hardly move and the Mouth was all parched and dry, while the Legs were unable to support the rest. So thus they found that even the Belly in its dull quiet way, was doing necessary work for the body and all must work together or the body will go to pieces."

The Belly, it seems, let the Members have their own way because it knew that they would come to their senses sooner or later when they discovered what it meant to be deprived of the blood and nourishment which it is the function of the Belly to supply.

It is quite superfluous to denote the lesson of this venerable fable further than to say that as the members of the individual human body are interdependent, so human beings in the mass are dependent upon one another for the things that make for health, happiness and a flourishing existence. Very often the man who does not seem to be doing his share of productive effort is in fact the most important link in the chain.

* * *

Consoled

She lay in his arms and snuggled her head against his neck * * * a rush of emotion surged through her * * * tenderly he caressed her and she closed her eyes in delight.

"Poor kitty. Did I step on your tail?"—

The Kiss of Love

IN NATURE the hills kiss heaven, the winds the forests, the waves the shore.

Lovely woman was made to be kissed, and loving man was made to kiss her.

People who say "no" to kisses either lie, are poorly constructed, or are in the unhappy class of old maids or misanthropes.

A kiss is Love's trademark and may be the bliss of heaven or the blister of hell.

There are all sorts of kisses—hot and cold, wet and dry, kind and cruel, short and long, friendly and false, pure and lascivious—some, like cement, bind hearts together; others, like dynamite, blow them up.

A kiss is either a prelude of blessed love or of burning lust.

Better kiss a red hot stove-lid than the painted lip of a heartless woman.

Cleopatra's passionate kiss destroyed Anthony's kingdom; Judas' kiss betrayed Christ; Joseph's kiss forgave his brethren; and the kiss of Benjamin West's mother made him an artist.

A married man should cultivate in the home the kissing habit he had when he courted. He should kiss his wife and children always, his mother-in-law occasionally, his servant, stenographer and neighbor's wife, never.

A girl should make her lips an altar of incense and not a fool's paradise.

She had better kiss a thoroughbred lap-dog than an ill-bred dancing dude.

Kisses are too sacred and valuable to throw away.

Deserve a kiss before you give or get one.

In Plato's day a war hero, young or old, could claim a kiss from every woman—today mere chocolate heroes are kissed for nothing.

Don't kiss in public—it's nauseating, not nice.

Don't kiss on street corners and block traffic; in depot and delay trains; in carriage and auto lest you confuse the driver; in canoe for fear of upsetting; and never make a public park a dove-cote in which to bill and coo.

A city license based on character should be required of persistent public spooners, and they should be quarantined from the cold-hearted public and watched over by an unjealous policeman who can sympathize with love's young dream, and crack a smile and not a scowl every time they kiss.

* * *

Time and the Man

Lady (to girl removing roll from the "first national bank)—"How do you get at your money, may I ask, when there are gentlemen about?"

Chorus Girl—"When there are gentlemen about I don't have to get at my money."

The Fable of a Skirt

There once was a Beautiful Bandit who was possessed of a pair of black eyes, a soprano voice and a stylish skirt which clung to Her understanding like the hangman's knot.

Now it happened that a certain Herbert Boyd was chasing his Dogs down the Main Drag of fast and fair New Yawk, with his kick full of kale when the Beautiful Bandit smote his tympanum with the soloful command of "hold 'em up." Behind the soprano voice was a business-like "gat."

Herbie was not a member of the Suicide Club and he had been Broke oftener than the ten commandments, so he carefully and quickly followed directions. The dark-eyed damsel thereupon frisked Herbie for fair and beat it with his roll. Herbie raised a great hue and cry, arousing the slumbering minions of the law.

The Beautiful Bandit then went away from there, but was hampered below the waist by the decree of fashion, which made her run like a Republican in Texas. She and her entire caste were hailed to the "hoosegow." Herbie allowed as how he had as much chance as a watermelon at an Alabama sangerfest had not the tight and stylish skirt come to his aid.

MORAL: There ain't any—it was positively im-MORAL.

* * *

Better a burning kiss than an unburned love letter.

Advice to the Species

By G. J. Liebst.

To those on paths of love who've lost their way
Come lend your ears to what I have to say;
My message brings to aching hearts surcease
From pain, while hunger-love I will appease.

Drink deep my words, then make another start—
The secret of success I will impart:
Come, would-be lovers for the truth athirst,
The men can wait, I'll speak to woman first:

To paraphrase the cook—here is my plan:
To meet success, you first must catch the man
That you desire, though give him not a clew,
But make him think that he is catching you.

Men like the chase, and when he thinks you caught,
Be not too fond, act like you think he's naught;
A little coldness now and then secures
His love, and soon you'll find that he is yours.

Who yields too soon, will soon her lover lose
Would you retain him long, then long refuse
His pleas for kisses, deftly turn aside—
Man fights for that of which he is denied.

As skillful riders rein with different force
The outlaw broncho and the well-trained horse,
You'll find the methods that will please old age
Will put the strippling youth in fiery rage.

Be careful of the tactics you employ.
What wins with man will oft repulse the boy;
The youthful flame is bright but sooner dies,
Make haste and sieze the love that swiftly flies.

The love in men of years, like dampened peat
Burns slowly but much longer retains heat,
And as the race of life draws near its goal,
You still may linger round the glowing coal.

Go now and to the male display your charms
And soon you find a pair of loving arms—
My rules have brought results since time began,
Go, try them out, I'll speak a word to man.

First, men, believe all women may be won,
When thus you start half of the work is done,
Make up your mind none can resist your skill
And she will yield who swears she never will.

Ask not for kisses, such a plea she'll spurn,
But take them (proper moments you will learn)
When once you've taken one she'll give you more
For fear of losing what you took before.

Be sparse with gifts, 'tis easy to bewitch
A female mind with promise made rich—
Who gives is mad, but make her still believe
The gift wil lcome, and thus success achieve.

Speak of her lovely face, her smile so sweet,
Praise every finger, and her little feet;
Such line of talk each woman loves to hear—
Both maid and matron hold their beauty dear.

Now in my school you've taken your degree
And learned the rudiments of love from me,
Fear not a shrinking woman to beguile—
The gods above forgive you with a smile.

* * *

They Answered Him

He had only ten dollars left and thought he would have a tour on the railway. So he hied himself to big ticket office where there was a host of booking clerks and inquired:

"Here. Can I go to Halifax for ten dollars?"

"No," answered the booking clerk.

"Well, can I have a return to Montreal?"

"No," replied the clerk again.

"Well, where can I go for ten dollars?" Then in a chorus they all answered him.

* * *

There is always a chance for a blind woman; she can qualify as a chaperon.

Wahoo. Blam. Blam!

Modern dance music is fascinating. It is called jazz, and is produced as follows: Five fellows, who cannot read music, are given five different pieces to play at once. They are equipped with a razzo, a bazzo, a blam blam, a wahoo, and a wheezer. They are then filled with Jamaica ginger, barbed wire, rough on rats, rock salt, home brew, and then turned loose. The noise that results is jazz. When people hear it, they say "they could die dancing." Many of them do, and the rest should. Just when they made delirium tremens unconstitutional, jazz came along and gave us dancing tremens. Guy now drinks a few bars of music and gets jazz instead of jag.

Nobody knows where it came from and nobody knows where it's going. Reformers claim it came from and is going to the same place.

* * *

Sweet Revenge

The enraged mob had torn the clothes off the poor wretch. Then the mob tarred and feathered him, placed a rope around his neck, and dragged him through the streets. Then the rope was thrown over an arm of a telegraph pole and the victim was hoisted high in the air and left to hang there.

"What did this fellow do?" we asked a member of the mob.

"Do?" yelled the member of the mob. "What did he do? Why he's the man who invented near beer."

Gold Tooth Luke's Revenge

The following is the experience of our hop head friend, Gold-Tooth Luke Head, as related by his coke snuffing brother, M. T. Head. Let's all take a shot and join in the chorus.

BY M. T. HEAD

It must have been two o'clock when he suddenly arose, and removing his hat and coat, he informed her that he must go. "I can't see that it is any of your business," she said as the alarm clock struck half-past. She arose and rang for the butler. Presently the maid entered. "Put some more wood on the radiator, Janet, the air is unusually thick this evening."

Then all was quiet except for the snoring of the cat in its cradle at the head of the stairs. It seemed as if he would never come back. Each hour seemed a minute. Someone knocked on the door and slowly the window opened and she came running in. "What did you do with it?" he growled. "I don't think so," she replied. "Why, then, have you made me suffer for another's wrong?" he answered. Suddenly she burst into tears and with a cunning smile replied, "So am I."

This was too much for him. He struck a match, and lighting his flashlight, fled into the night. All was calm without; silence being broken only by the barking of flying fish, and the occasional quack of a wild poodle-dog.

Once in the woods, he forgot his troubles and gave orders to the cook to have the side curtains put up on the coupe. His chauffeur having been shot earlier in the evening, he must prepare his own dinner. He had planned on having bard-boiled eggplant, but alas, his matches were wet and he could not light the electric stove. He was alone in the wilderness without a match. Lighting a Fatima, he stretched out on the piano stool for a quiet nap, gazing lazily at the moonlit clouds below.

He had no more than closed one eye, when she came bursting in on tiptoes. Before she could stop him, he had gathered her up in his manly arms, and thus our little story comes to a happy ending.

* * *

Old Time Courting

"The young fellow of today does not know what courting means," declared ex-Speaker Cannon, discoursing on the trials of courting under the old regime.

"In the old days," continued he, "a young man would walk ten miles through the rain or snow, freeze his ears and fingers, and face the danger of wildcats to see his girl.

"And when he did see her it was in the general living room, with the rest of the family present. The men who courted in these conditions know what courting was.

"Divorce was not the popular pastime then

as it is now. Those couples stuck through thick and thin, obeying the scriptural injunction that what God hath joined together no man shall put asunder.

"All the courting was on Sunday night and it was a ceremony religiously observed. The swain remained at his sweetheart's home until after midnight, even though the rest of the family sat up with him.

"When he went home through the storm or in the bright starlight, he walked the earth as a conqueror, for he had been in the presence that to him represented the real poem of life. He would stick to her and she to him through life.

"Some of the old fashions have never been improved upon, and one of them is the old-fashioned courting."

There is a lot of truth in Uncle Joe's assertions. New fashioned flirting, combined with the jazz bands, accounts for the slump in wedding bells.

The love bug finds it impossible to bite a man who's jumping to the syncopations of the "jazz." So now balls are arranged with a waltz or two thrown in here and there just to give Cupid a look in.

The match-making mamma has lots of advice to give to her daughter. "My dear, when Lord Shirkitt asks you for a dance, be sure to make it a waltz. Don't dance any of those silly fox trot or one-step things with him, for he's the nicest young man in London and has a bigger bank account than anyone I know."

And the dutiful daughter spends an unhappy but tense evening in the dressing room, listening through all the ragtime monstrosities for the welcome uplifting strains of a dreamy waltz.

Then she floats into the dancing ring. Shirkitt floats out of single blessedness.

* * *

Proof

A college student had a barrel of ale deposited in his room, contrary, of course, to rule and usage. He received a summons to appear before the college president.

"Sir, I am informed that you have a barrel of ale in your room," said the latter.

"Yes, sir."

"What explanation can you make?"

"Why, the fact is, sir, my physician advises me to try a little each day as a tonic, and not wishing to go to the various places where the beverage is retailed, I arranged to have a barrel in my room."

"Indeed. And have you derived any benefit from the use of it?"

"Oh, yes, sir. When the barrel was first taken to my room I could scarcely lift it. Now I can carry it easily."

* * *

The unholy trinity—Moonshine—Moonlight—Maiden.

* * *

A pug nose sometimes gives a man a dogged expression.

A Maiden's Prayer

She doesn't go down on her knees as a rule,
Not unless she's wearing lisle tops.
But it's none the less devout.
It goes something like this:
I say, Fate, Old Bean.
I pray you make me as unto a preacherino.
You know what I mean.

AS NEAR to the standard recently set up by a New York impressario on the lookout for Beauty as you can conveniently manage.

To prevent you from bungling, I'll just append it for you herewith:

* * * the bewildering beauty of a summer's night, high moon and the melodious voice of a half-awakened mocking bird calling to its mate, and tresses as sparkling as dew bespangled flowers alight with the flame of a lying sun.

* * * all the physical virtues of Petrarch's Laura, Annie Laurie, burning Sappho, Heloise, and Helen of Troy.

I should really be awfully obliged, old thing, if that could be arranged.

It would mean so much to me. Not only should I get my picture served up with all the world's editions, but I should be enabled to earn enough money to keep my dependents in luxury and myself real silk stockinged to the grave.

But if you won't make me fair—at least make me wise.

With the wisdom that can detect the Cotton Back, the Padded Shoulders, the de-Tecla kind of pearls, and the Tinned Peaches of Life.

And you might give me, too, neatness in my figure, my ankles, my dexterity with the lobster pick, my prowess at the tickle toe, my handling of asparagus or of any of the Great Minority that domes my way.

Bless me also with a good complexion.

One that no sun, seawater, pastries, rich food, tears (crocodile and otherwise) can harm.

Failing this, let me be lucky enough to hit on a suitable powder—one that sticketh closer than a brother, one that will take the shine out of the worst regulated nose, and above all, one that doesn't show.

And perhaps, one day I'll be lucky enough to find a really successful hair curler.

A really comfortable pair of corsets.

A really clever and cheap dressmaker.

A boot shop which won't let its assistants argue when I want to ge a one shoe on to the two foot.

And if I can't persuade you to make a Mary Pickford of me or give me the taking ways which will win a golden pippin.

It wouldn't hurt you to let me bring down a matrimonial plum.

But, mind you, I don't want him too plump,

or over-ripe, or the least little bit stony about the pockets.

And if he doesn't possess a passbook which passeth all misunderstanding, do please, dear old fatey, see that he's one of those $100,000-a-year-job-young men.

And that he gets the job.

And you might make sure he's one of those model husbands which you hear tell about but never see on exhibition.

He must be a chap who will always admire me, even when I've been crying or have mislaid my powder puff, and he mustn't go off the deep end in the bathroom whenever I cut the corns with his best razor.

And he mustn't mind toast crumbs, because I like to have my breakfast in bed when I feel off color.

And, I say, fate-ums, I should adore a couple of nice children—

Who will never talk with their mouths full, or refuse to run upstairs for me, or bang doors, or interfere with my things, or put their fingers into anything or fall down the coal-hole, or get whooping cough, the mumps, or cut off their curls, or drink my hair oil, or hit the kids next door with anything heavier than the clothes prop.

And I should so like the boy to grow up and take me on his knees just as nicely as does Robert Loraine in "Mary Rose."

And the girl to say, with a filial sigh, "How beeutiful you were, Ma, in those days."

You don't know how grateful I would be if you could wangle all this, O Fate.

And if you do decide in the affirmative you might get a move on as quickly as possible.

I've been waiting so long.

And I'm so fed up with my present personal estate.

Main items being: A shiny nose and an aching heart.

* * *

Embellishing Kisses

A kiss fairly electrifies you; no language expresses it. A kiss is as old as creation; Eve learned it in Paradise, and was taught its beauties, virtues, and varieties by an angel, for there is something so transcendent in it.—Clyde.

* * *

Kissing an unwilling pair of lips is as mean a victory as robbing a bird's nest, and kissing too willing ones is about as unfragrant a recreation as making bouquets out of dandelions.—J. Brientnall.

* * *

The soul of a young woman is a ripe rose; as soon as one leaf is plucked, all its mates easily fall after; and a kiss may sometimes break out the first leaf.—Mrs. John Sanford.

* * *

In every grade of society there is kissing; go where you will, to what country you will, you are perfectly sure to find kissing.—R. Griffiths.

Formation of Women

ANCIENT mythology and folklore contain innumerable stories of the creation of the world and of man. Most of them have this in common that they relate that, when it came to the creation of woman, the being who had the task in hand experienced immense difficulties. According to a supposed legend, for instance, this is the origin of woman:

"Twashtri, the god Vulcan of the Hindu mythology, created the world, but on his commencing to create woman he discovered that for man he had exhausted all his creative materials, and that not one element had been left. This, of course, greatly perplexed Twashtri, and caused him to fall into a profound meditation. When he arose from it he proceeded as follows:

He took:

The roundness of the moon.

The undulating curve of the serpent.

The graceful twist of the creeping plant.

The light shivering of the grass blade and the slenderness of the willow.

The velvet of the flowers.

The lightness of the feather.

The gentle gaze of the doe.

The frolicsomeness of the dancing sunbeam.

The tears of the cloud.
The inconsistency of the wind.
The timidity of the hare.
The vanity of the peacock.
The hardness of the diamond.
The cruelty of the tiger.
The chill of the snow.
The cackling of the parrot.
The cooing of the turtle dove.

All these he mixed together and formed a woman."

This is widely accepted as an ancient Hindu legend and nobody would suffer very much for continuing to believe such to be the case, but a gentleman, in answer to a query the other day, completely destroys the foundations for this belief. He says: "The legend of the creation of woman is the creation in English of an English mind; its author is F. W. Bain, and it is to be found in his charming book, 'A Digit of the Moon.'"

* * *

Fable of the Jawbone

Once upon a time there was a tramp who was hungry. He "Hit it up" to a back door of a hospitable, home-looking house.

"Can you give a rotten, old bum a handout?" he queried.

"My good man, certainly I'll give you something to eat, but why talk so roughly?" replied the good housekeeper. "Don't you know that you would be lots better off in this world if you practiced the teachings of your mother? I'll give you something to eat, and in the meantime while I'm preparing your meal I'll tell you a Bible story.

"Once upon a time there was a strong man by the name of Samson. He slew ten thousand Philistines with the jawbone of an ass and stole the gates of Jerusalem. Wasn't he a strong man?"

Two weeks later the same "bum" became ravenously hungry again. His "feeds" had been few and far between. He was still in the same village. He thought of the same story of the good old lady. Hunger was on him and his thoughts centered on the story of Samson. He promptly hied himself to the favored house. He knocked at the door and his motherly friend answered.

"My good woman, if you will please give me something to eat, I will tell you a Bible story.

She, being religiously inclined, was glad to listen to his recital of Biblical days. "Certainly, poor man, I am pleased to hear your story," she said. "Go ahead."

Once upon a time there was a strong man by the name of Sam Thompson. He slew ten thousand Philadelphians with the jawbone of an ass and stole the gates of New Jersey; now wasn't he a go-get-'em son-of-a-gun?"

* * *

There is much virtue in a kiss well delivered.—Sidney Smith.

* * *

How rapturous is the kiss of honest love.—W. Godwin.

Poppies

BY J. EUGENE CHRISMAN

Poppies?
Not for me, buddy!
Buds o' Hell I'd call 'em,
Plain red hell—they—
They remind me—

And folks plant 'em around
Gardens—huh!
Says one old dame to me,
"Don't they bring back," says she,
"The poppied fields of Flanders?"
"Poppied fields of—" ain't that a heluva—
But who wants 'em brung back—huh?
Say, buddy,
If she'd seen poppies
Like I've seen 'em—millions—acres—
Scattered through the wheat-fields,
Red—and gettin' redder—mostly poppies—

Slim—my buddy—old scout
Slept under the same handkerchief,
Me 'n' Slim—clean through from the word go!
I'm liable to forgit—ain't I—
Day we kicked off west o' Chateau-Thierry
Down the valley—
Poppies—say,
You couldn't rest for poppies.
Then the Jerries cut loose
Machine-gun fire—reg'lar sickle.
Poppy leaves—bits o' red
Flickin' and flutterin' in the wind,
Mowed 'em, buddy—and us—I'll tell the world!
Got old Slim—got him right!
Down in the poppies he goes—kickin'—clawin'!
Don't talk poppies to me—
Skunk cabbage first—compree?
If you'd seen old Slim—
Boy, he died wallerin' in poppies!
Poppies—
Hell!

* * *

Acme of human happiness is that we may kiss whom we please, and please whom we kiss.
—Miss F. Prichard.

Embellishing Beauty

Beauty is a fairy; sometimes she hides herself in a flower cup, or under a leaf, or creeps into the old ivy, and plays hide and seek with the sunbeams, or haunts some ruined spot, or laughs out of a bright young face.—Sala.

* * *

There should be, methinks, as little merit in loving a woman for her beauty as in loving a man for his prosperity; both being equally subject to change.—Pope.

* * *

Beauty in a modest woman is like fire at a distance, or like a sharp word; neither doth the one burn, nor the other wound those that come not too near them.—Cervantes.

* * *

Nature has given horns to bulls, hoofs to horses, swiftness to hares, the power of swimming to fishes, of flying to birds, understanding to men. She had nothing more for women. What then does she give? Beauty, which can resist shields and spears; she who is beautiful is stronger than iron and fire.—Anacreon.

* * *

Beauty is a dangerous property, tending to corrupt the mind of the wife, though it soon loses its influence over the husband; a figure agreeable and engaging, which inspires affection, without the ebriety of love is a much safer choice.—Lord Kames.

* * *

Beauty has been the delight and torment of the world ever since it began; the philosophers have felt its influences so sensibly that almost every one of them has left some saying or other which intimated that he knew too well the power of it.—Steele.

* * *

A smooth, soft, and transparent skin, is no less indispensable to the perfection of beauty than elegance of figure; it is, indeed, the barometer of the health and soundness of the individual, and the most indubitable sign of true beauty.—Sir J. Clark.

* * *

Moral beauty is the basis of all true beauty. This foundation is somewhat covered and veiled in nature; art brings it out, and gives it more transparent forms. It is here that art, when it knows well its powers and resources, engages in a struggle with nature in which it may have the advantage.—Cousin.

* * *

Beauty is the true prerogative of women, and so peculiarly their own, that our sex, though naturally requiring another sort of feature, is never in its luster but when puerile and beardless, confused and mixed with theirs.—Montaigne.

Our Rural Mail Box

My Urez—There is as much difference between a Hootannanny and a Whiffanpoof as there is between a Muffleguzzer and a Lollapoloozer. Hope that will satisfy you.

* * *

Count Adenoid, Duluth—You say you suffer from cold feet. This is due to poor circulation, and as we advised before, you ought to take a walk, visiting all of your friends' homes, and boost for the Whiz Bang. This is sure to increase the circulation.

* * *

Fuller Wholes—What's the big idea? You ask me why a marriage ceremony is like a hunkacheese, and then you proceed to answer it yourself, thusly: "I don't know, unless it's cuz they're both binding!"

* * *

Mrs. Bee—To entertain your lady callers, let them inspect your husband's private correspondence.

* * *

Authoress—We are overloaded at present with stories of newly married couples. Come again! Give us your address, we might take a trip to Duluth some day. Thanks for the photo.

Newlywed—A little Portland cement added to oatmeal while boiling will give it the body desired.

* * *

Poet—Sorry, we can't use your peppery poem. If you have a hair-raising story, tell it to some bald-headed man.

* * *

Betty B. Good—Don't complain that your confidence has been betrayed. The fault is your own for pouring unsafe talk into a leaky mind.

* * *

Tonsorialist—I predict a great future for you in the barber business. You are bound to be at the head.

* * *

Hobo B No. 2—You are right. When one hasn't eaten for seven days, that makes one weak.

* * *

Buddy—Just so, but the poet had only Mademoiselle from Armentieres' word for it. Forty years is a long time, you know!

* * *

Casey—When making a call at a private house, do not keep harping on the good old days when one could get a shot of booze. It is exceedingly bad form.

* * *

Jane—If you must eat onions, for land's sake, Jane, don't breathe it to a soul.

* * *

Ella Gant—Spices as a rule are not noisy, but beware of ginger snaps.

Pious Yank Soldiers

I AM going to tell you a story—an honest-to-goodness true story and no bathroom rumor.

At Winchester, England, there was a so-called "rest " camp for American soldiers who passed through that country to or from France. At this camp there also was a huge Y. M. C. A. "auditorium" tent, seating several thousand persons.

Near the stage were hundreds of chairs. The back of the "arena" had boards for seats, and due to English rains, the back seats usually had a thick coating of "limey" mud. As a result, there always was an early rush for the front chairs.

One evening in November, 1918, while stationed at a convalescent camp near Winchester, my buddy and I journeyed to the big tent an hour early so as to get the choice seats. Evangeline Booth, of the Salvation Army, was booked to speak.

We were stopped in the aisles and told to take a back seat, because the front chairs had been reserved for a group of seventy-five "Y" workers. About two hundred soldiers disagreed with the ushers and we made a grand rush for the front chairs, bowling over the attendant as we passed onward.

The secretary in charge pleaded for order "Now, men, I know we have agreed not to hol any religious meetings except on Sundays, bu as Mrs. Booth is to be here tonight, I thinl we ought to sing a hymn."

Then, as the organist started to play "On ward Christian Soldiers," a deep voice at th rear piped: "All we do is sign the payroll,' and the tune spread like wildfire.

"All we do is sign the payroll, and we neve get a gosh darned cent," with emphasis on th "G. D."

The secretary was horrified. He tremble like a French M'amselle doing a parlor shimmy He begged and pleaded for order, and finall the song died away to be followed immediatel by the old marching song:

"Poilu, have you a daughter fair,
"Parley Vouz.
"Poilu, have you a daughter fair,
"Parley Vouz.
"Poilu, have you a daughter fair,
"With lily white cheeks
"And goldcn hair.
"Hinky Pinky, Parley Vouz."

Again and again the mighty song resounde until suddenly a wild-eyed and much excite Englishman, in a Salvation Army uniform rushed on the stage from the wings. His dramatic entrance silenced the singers.

"Oah, Oah, I say, old chappie," he exclaimed "Mrs. Booth's car is stuck in the mud, Mrs Booth's car is stuck in the mud. Give me fift men at once, my dear sir, Mrs. Booth's car is stuck in the mud."

"Aw, send a couple of Yanks," shouted somebody at the rear. The crowd laughed good-naturedly and several Yanks responded to the call to help Mrs. Booth out of the mud-marooned automobile.

Her entrance hushed the "rebels" and the vociferous applause plainly indicated the appreciation of the Yanks toward the Salvation Army.

* * *

A kiss is an alms which enriches him who receives without impoverishing her who gives. —Ninon de L'Enclos.

* * *

It is the passion that is in a kiss that gives to it its sweetness; it is the affection in a kiss that sanctifies it.—Bovee.

* * *

The kiss of a virtuous is sweeter than honey; the perfumes of Arabia breathe from her lips. —R. Dodsley.

* * *

A kiss is at once the token of boldness, confidence, and affection.—Niphus.

* * *

'Tis better to have loved and lost when you read of some of the mean things they say in the divorce court.

* * *

When the curtain in the theater takes a drop, some of the men go out to follow suit.

SEND NO MONEY!

5000 MILES OF SERVICE—We stand ready and willing to satisfy you and back up our iron bound 5000 Mile Adjustment Basis proposition. These are not "Double Treads" or "Rebuilt" tires, but first grade standard casings and others that have been slightly used. Some of them have been run less than 200 miles. **DON'T SEND US A CENT**—just write your order. Examine the tires when they arrive. If you want to keep them, pay the expressman. If not, send them back. New Tube Free With Every Tire. Order today at these prices. **TUBE FREE.**

30x3	$ 7.00	33x4	$11.75
30x3½	7.75	34x4	12.25
*32x3½	8.75	33x4½	13.25
31x4	9.75	34x4½	14.25
32x4	10.75	35x4½	15.25
32x4½	12.75	36x4½	15.50
*S. S. Only		37x5	16.50

When ordering state size and number wanted.

JEAN TIRE CO. (Not Inc.) Div. 13-G
2348 W. Harrison Street - CHICAGO

INSTRUCTIVE AND ENTERTAINING BOOKS

These are bound in attractive covers and cover many subjects.
PRICE, 25c EACH, POSTPAID, 5 FOR $1.00, or the entire set of 12 books for $2.00, P. P. Select from this list:

Boxing and Boating	Beauty Secrets
Oriental Dream Book	How to Dance
How to Pitch Ball	Lover's Secrets
Book of Birthdays	Rope Splicing
Guide to the Stage	Heller's Magic
Thurston's Card Tricks	Love Letters

J. C. Dorn 725 S. Dearborn St. Dept. 70-Chicago, Ill.

ROBUST HEALTH FOR MEN

For men who are run down, whose vitality is low, who have lost the spring in their muscles and the vim and vigor of healthy manhood, there is hope in a discovery made recently and now offered to the public.

RE-NU-TABS

A simple treatment based on a physician's prescription and used by thousands of physicians, is the greatest tablet made. It will bring back the feeling of masculine power to man who has lost his "punch." It is body building,—rejuvenating. It costs you nothing to learn about the treatment. Simply write, a card will do, to the

RE-NU LABORATORIES
Dept. V—Gateway Station,
Kansas City, Mo.

IF YOU want healthy, wealthy, loving wife, write Violet Rays, Dennison, Ohio. (stamp.)

PILES—Cured or No Pay $2 if cured. Remedy sent on trial. Send 10c for postage. Kuro Remedy Company, Dept. 33, Kansas City, Mo.

MEN!

Try my best Electric Belt with special sex invigorator. Free 60 days. Knocks rheumatism, stomach, kidney, bladder, prostatic weakness, n; greatest power; half price. Eye-opening facts free. A. P. Owens, Dept. B., P. O. Box 861, Indianapolis, Ind.

STAMMER

If you stammer attend no stammering school until you get my large FREE cloth bound book entitled "Stammering, Its Origin and The Advanced Natural Method of Cure." Ask for special tuition rate and a FREE copy of "The Natural Speech Magazine." Largest and best equipped and most successful school in the world for the cure of stammering. No sing-song or time beat. Write today. **School open all year. Now is the best time to enroll. The North-Western School, 2339 Grand Ave., Milwaukee, Wis.**

FREE for 10 Days' Wear

Send no money—just tell us which ring to send—No. 102 or 103. We will send you one of these genuine sparkling Tifnite gems mounted in solid gold—on 10 days' FREE TRIAL. Don't miss this offer. Send.

Put It Beside a Diamond When it arrives, deposit $3.50 with postmaster. Wear it 10 days. See how beautiful it is. **If anyone can tell it from a diamond, send it back and we refund deposit.** If you buy, pay the balance at $3.00 per month until $12.50 is paid. Write today. Send strip of paper fitting end to end around finger joint for ring size.

THE TIFNITE CO. 511 S. Plymouth Ct. Dept. 1924 Chicago

Your Skin can be Quickly Cleared of

PIMPLES

Blackheads, Acne Eruptions on the face or body, Enlarged Pores, Oily or Shiny Skin. Write today for my FREE booklet, "A CLEAR-TONE SKIN", telling how I cured myself after being afflicted 15 years. $1,000 Cold Cash says I can clear your skin of the above blemishes. **E. S. GIVENS, 207 Chemical Bldg., Kansas City, Mo.**

MOTOR DRIVEN **FREE TALKING MACHINE**

WE PAY CHARGES

PLAYS ALL STANDARD RECORDS INCLUDING 10 INCH

Handsome metal case, excellent motor. Prepaid for selling only 16 boxes Mentho-Nova Salve, the antiseptic Menthol Ointment. Sell at special price 25c. Return the $4.00 and this fine Phonograph is yours. Supply is limited. We trust you. Order today. Satisfaction guaranteed.

U. S. SUPPLY CO., DEPT. 400 GREENVILLE, PA.

CORRESPONDENT—Oldest and most reliable club; make acquaintances everywhere, Box 85, Toledo, Ohio.

STOP TOBACCO HABIT!—Simply send name today for Free sample famous Tobacco Boon. No craving for tobacco, any form, after first few doses. Dr. H. Will Elders, Dept. 1011, St. Joseph, Mo.

ECZEMA

IS CURABLE. Write me today and I will send you a free trial of my mild, soothing guaranteed treatment that will prove it. Stops the itching and heals permanently. Dr. Cannaday, Park Square, Sedalia, Missouri. **1952.**

MEN ON THE DOWN GRADE who are losing out in life, caused from weak, nervous, despondent, run down condition, take Castleberry's Pills. They accomplish marvelous results and possess wonderful rejuvenating forces. Mail, $1.00. Three boxes $2.75. Six boxes $5.00. Sample and testimonials free. A. F. Castleberry, Box 564, Columbus, Georgia.

$5,000 YEARLY INCOME

Paid Thousands of people who invested in Texas Oil lands. They made the start. $2 may start you making $200 monthly, possibly more. You get warranty deed to land with interest in entire sub-division. Results count. Bank reference, established facts free. Write today. Sourlake Texas Oil Co., 626 Demenil, St. Louis, Mo.

CURED HIS RHEUMATISM

"I am eighty-three years old and I doctored for rheumatism ever since I came out of the army, over 50 years ago. Like many others, I spent money freely for so-called 'cures' and I have read about 'Uric Acid' until I could almost taste it. I could not sleep nights or walk without pain; my hands were so sore and stiff I could not hold a pen. But now I am again in active business and can walk with ease or write all day with comfort. Friends are surprised at the change." You might just as well attempt to put out a fire with oil as try to get rid of your rheumatism, neuritis and like complaints by taking treatment supposed to drive Uric Acid out of your blood and body. It took Mr. Ashelman fifty years to find out the truth. He learned how to get rid of the true cause of his rheumatism, other disorders, and recover his strength from "The Inner Mysteries," now being distributed free by an authority who devoted over twenty years to the scientific study of this trouble. If any reader of the "Whiz Bang" wishes "The Inner Mysteries of Rheumatism" overlooked by doctors and scientists for centuries past, simply send a post card or letter to H. P. Clearwater, No. 1259-A St., Hallowell, Maine. Send now, lest you forget! If not a sufferer, cut out this notice and hand this good news and opportunity to some afflicted friend. All who send will receive it by return mail without any charge whatever.

YOU HAVE A BEAUTIFUL FACE

BUT YOUR NOSE?

BEFORE AFTER

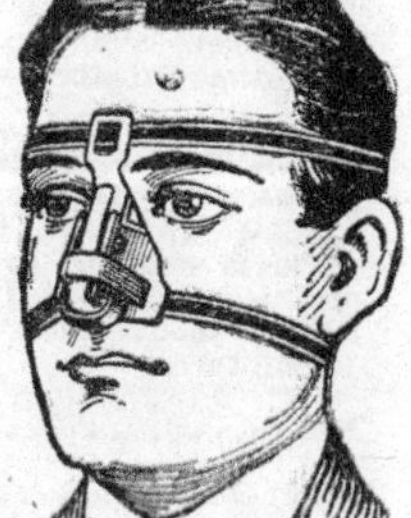

In this day and age attention to your appearance is an absolute necessity if you expect to make the most out of life. Not only should you wish to appear as attractive as possible, for your own self satisfaction, which is alone well worth your efforts, but you will find the world in general judging you greatly, if not wholly, by your "looks," therefore it pays to "look your best" at all times. **Permit no one to see you looking otherwise;** it will injure your welfare! Upon the impression you constantly make rests the failure or success of your life. Which is to be your ultimate destiny? My latest Nose Shaper, "Trados Model 25," U. S. Patent, with six adjustable pressure regulators and made of light polished metal, corrects now ill-shaped noses without operation, quickly, safely and permanently. Diseased cases excepted. Does not interfere with one's work, being worn at night.

Write today for free booklet, which tells you how to correct ill-shaped noses without cost if not satisfactory.

M. TRILETY, Face Specialist **1607 Ackerman Bldg., Binghamton, N. Y.**

Also for Sale at Riker-Hegeman, Liggett's, and other first-class drug stores.

Join the Family

Capt. Billy's Whiz Bang employs no solicitors. Subscriptions may be received only at authorized news stands or by direct mail to Robbinsdale. We join in no clubbing offers, nor do we give premiums. This is done to protect YOU from the horde of magazine swindlers scattered all over the United States. If your news dealer hasn't been able to supply you regularly with the monthly issue of the Whiz Bang, don't blame him. The demand has usually exceeded the supply at every news stand in the country and if you have experienced trouble and would prefer to have the magazine delivered to your home or your hotel, send us two dollars and a half and we will see that you get it each month. Subscribers get the first copies off the press and changes in addresses are recorded within forty-eight hours after their receipt at Robbinsdale. Fill out the coupon below and mail to us.

Subscribe Now

If you like our Farmyard Filosophy and Foolishness, fill in this coupon.

$2.50
For 12 Issues
$3.50 with Annual

Capt. Billy's Whiz Bang,
R. R. 2, Robbinsdale, Minn.

Enclosed is money order (or check) for subscription commencing with........................issue
MONTH

Name..................................

Street..................................

City & State..................................

(Original inside front cover ad)

Remember Your Friends!

When you have finished reading this Annual and if you have enjoyed it and think that it is worthy of a place in your book case as a memento to be cherished in after years, remember your friends need cheering up.

We'll Mail It!

Fill out the attached coupon and append to it a one dollar bill or check, money order or stamps for one dollar, and write in the address of the person to whom you wish the annual sent, on the coupon; mail to us and we will forward without delay a Winter Annual, "Pedigreed Follies of 1921-22," to the lucky one.

CAPTAIN BILLY'S WHIZ BANG

Robbinsdale, Minnesota

Gentlemen:

Enclosed is $1.00, check, money order or stamps, for which please send the Winter Annual of Capt. Billy's Whiz Bang, "Pedigreed Follies of 1921-22," to the following address:

Name ....

Address ....

(Please acknowledge receipt of this order to the following address:)

My name..

My address..

(Original inside back cover ad)

Made in the USA
Monee, IL
27 January 2024

52483652R00152